Eight
Pillars *of*
Prosperity

JAMES ALLEN TITLES

———○◦•◦○———

Eight Pillars *of* Prosperity

James Allen

MEDIA

Published 2019 by Gildan Media LLC
aka G&D Media
www.GandDmedia.com

Design by Meghan Day Healey of Story Horse, LLC

Library of Congress Cataloging-in-Publication Data is available upon request

ISBN: 978-1-7225-0251-5

10   9   8   7   6   5   4   3   2   1

He who would build both strong and high
        Must first of all dig deep and low;
        So rose the spire against the sky,
And so doth skill and knowledge grow.
        So, with well-ordered strenuousness,
        Raise thou thy structure of Success.

Contents

Preface

I t is popularly supposed that a greater prosperity
for individuals or nations can only come through
a political and social reconstruction. This cannot
be true apart from the practice of the moral virtues in the individuals that comprise a nation. Better laws and social conditions will always follow a
higher realization of morality among the individuals of a community, but no legal enactment can
give prosperity to, nay, it cannot prevent the ruin
of, a man or a nation that has become lax and decadent in the pursuit and practice of virtue.

The moral virtues are the foundation and support of prosperity as they are the soul of greatness.
They endure forever, and all the works of man
which endure are built upon them. Without them
there is neither strength, stability, nor substantial

reality, but only ephemeral dreams. To find moral principles is to have found prosperity, greatness, truth, and is therefore to be strong, valiant, joyful, and free.

—James Allen
Bryngoleu,
Ilfracombe, England

The Eight Pillars

Prosperity rests upon a moral foundation. It is popularly supposed to rest upon an immoral foundation—that is, upon trickery, sharp practice, deception, and greed. One commonly hears even an otherwise intelligent man declare that "No man can be successful in business unless he is dishonest;" thus regarding business prosperity, a good thing, as the effect of dishonesty, a bad thing. Such a statement is superficial and thoughtless, and reveals a total lack of knowledge of moral causation, as well as a very limited grasp of the facts of life. It is as though one should sow henbane and reap spinach, or erect a brick house on a quagmire,—things impossible in the natural order of causation, and therefore not to be attempted. The spiritual or moral order of causation is not different in principle, but only in nature. The same law obtains in things unseen—in thoughts and deeds—as in things seen—in natural phenomena. Man sees the processes in natural objects, and acts in accordance with them, but not seeing the spiritual processes, he imagines that they do not obtain, and so he does not act in harmony with them.

Yet these spiritual processes are just as simple and just as sure as the natural processes. They are indeed the same *natural* modes manifesting in the world of mind. All the parables and a large number of the sayings of the Great Teachers are designed to illustrate this fact. The natural world is the mental world made visible. The seen is the mirror of the unseen. The upper half of a circle is in no way different from the lower half, but its sphericity is reversed. The material and the mental are not two detached arcs in the universe, they are the two halves of a complete circle. The natural and the spiritual are not at eternal enmity, but in the true order of the universe are eternally at one. It is in the *unnatural*—in the abuse of function and faculty—where division arises, and where man is wrested back, with repeated sufferings, from the perfect circle from which he has tried to depart. Every process in matter is also a process in mind. Every natural law has its spiritual counterpart.

Take any natural object, and you will find its fundamental processes in the mental sphere if you rightly search. Consider, for instance, the germination of a seed and its growth into a plant with the final development of a flower, and back to seed again. This also is a mental process. Thoughts are seeds which, falling in the soil of the mind, germinate and develop until they reach the completed stage, blossoming into deeds good or bad, brilliant or stupid, according to their nature, and ending as seeds of thought to be again sown in other minds. A teacher is a sower of seed, a spiritual agriculturist, while he who teaches himself is the wise farmer of his own mental plot. The growth of a thought is as the growth of a plant. The seed must be sown seasonably, and time is required for its full development into the plant of knowledge and the flower of wisdom.

While writing this, I pause and turn to look through my study window, and there, a hundred yards away, is a tall tree in the top of which some enterprising rook from a rookery hard by has, for the first time, built its nest. A strong northeast wind is blowing, so that the top of the tree is swayed violently to and fro by the onset of the blast; yet there is no danger to that frail thing of sticks and hair, and the mother bird, sitting upon her eggs, has no fear of the storm. Why is this? It is because the bird has instinctively built her nest in harmony with principles which ensure the maximum strength and security. First a fork is chosen as the foundation for the nest, and not a space between two separate branches, so that however great may be the swaying of the tree-top, the position of the nest is not altered, nor its structure disturbed; then the nest is built on a circular plan so as to offer the greatest resistance to any external pressure, as well as to obtain more perfect compactness within, in accordance with its purpose; and so, however the tempest may rage, the birds rest in comfort and security. This is a very simple and familiar object, and yet, in the strict obedience of its structure to mathematical law, it becomes, to the wise, a parable of enlightenment, teaching them that only by ordering one's deeds in accordance with fixed principles is perfect surety, perfect security, and perfect peace obtained amid the uncertainty of events and the turbulent tempests of life.

A house or a temple built by man is a much more complicated structure than a bird's nest, yet it is erected in accordance with those mathematical principles which are everywhere evidenced in nature. And here is seen how man, in material things, obeys universal principles. He never attempts to put up a building in defiance of geometrical proportions, for he knows that such a building would be unsafe, and that the first storm would, in all probability, level it to the ground, if, indeed, it did not fall about his ears during the process of erection. Man in his material building scrupulously obeys the fixed principles of circle, square, and angle, and aided by rule, plumb-line, and compasses, he raises a structure which will resist the fiercest storms, and afford him a secure shelter and safe protection.

All this is very simple, the reader may say. Yes, it is simple because it is true and perfect; so true that it cannot admit the smallest compromise, and so perfect that no man can improve upon it. Man, through long experience, has learned these princi-ples of the material world, and sees the wisdom of obeying them, and I have thus referred to them in order to lead up to a consideration of those fixed principles in the mental or spiritual world which are just as simple, and just as eternally true and perfect, yet are at present so little understood by man that he daily violates them, because ignorant of their nature, and unconscious of the harm he is all the time inflicting upon himself.

In mind as in matter, in thoughts as in things, in deeds as in natural processes, there is a fixed foundation of law which, if consciously or igno-rantly ignored, leads to disaster and defeat. It is, indeed, the ignorant violation of this law which is the cause of the world's pain and sorrow. In matter, this law is presented as *mathematical*; in mind, it is perceived as *moral*. But the mathematical and the moral are not separate and opposed; they are but two aspects of a united whole. The fixed principles of mathematics, to which all matter is subject, are the body of which the spirit is ethical; while the eternal principles of morality are mathematical truisms operating in the universe of mind. It is as impossible to live successfully apart from moral principles, as to build successfully while ignoring mathematical principles. Characters, like houses, only stand firmly when built on a foundation of moral law,—and they are built up slowly and laboriously, deed by deed, for in the building of character, the bricks are deeds. Businesses and all human enterprises are not exempt from the eternal order, but can only stand securely by the observance of fixed laws. Prosperity, to be stable and enduring, must rest on a solid foundation of moral principle, and be supported by the adamantine pillars of sterling character and moral worth. In the attempt to run a business in defiance of moral principles, disaster, of one kind or another, is inevitable. The permanently prosperous men in any community are not its tricksters and deceivers, but its reliable and upright men. The Quakers are acknowledged to be the most upright men in the British community, and, although their numbers are small, they are the most prosperous. The Jains in India are similar both in numbers and sterling worth, and they are the most prosperous people in India.

Men speak of "building up a business," and, indeed, a business is as much a building as is a brick house or a stone church, albeit the process of building is a mental one. Prosperity, like a house, is a roof over a man's head, affording him protection and comfort. A roof presupposes a support, and a support necessitates a foundation. The roof of prosperity, then, is supported by the following eight pillars which are cemented in a foundation of moral consistency:

1. Energy.
2. Economy.
3. Integrity.
4. System.
5. Sympathy.
6. Sincerity.
7. Impartiality.
8. Self-reliance.

A business built up on the faultless practice of all these principles would be so firm and enduring as to be invincible. Nothing could injure it; nothing could undermine its prosperity; nothing could interrupt its success, or bring it to the ground;

but that success would be assured with incessant increase so long as the principles were adhered to. On the other hand, where these principles were all absent, there could be no success of any kind; there could not even be a business at all, for there would be nothing to produce the adherence of one part with another; but there would be that lack of life, that absence of fibre and consistency, which animates and gives body and form to any object whatsoever. Picture a man with all these principles absent from his mind, his daily life, and even if your knowledge of these principles is but slight and imperfect, yet you could not think of such a man as doing any successful work. You could picture him as leading the confused life of a shiftless tramp, but to imagine him at the head of a business, as the centre of an organization, or as a responsible and controlling agent in any department of life—this you could not do, because you realize its impossibility. The fact that no one of moderate morality and intelligence can think of such a man as commanding any success, should, to all those who have not yet grasped the import of these principles and therefore declare that morality is not a factor, but rather a hindrance, in prosperity, be a sound proof to them that their conclusion is totally wrong; for if it was right, then the greater the lack of these moral principles, the greater would be the success.

These eight principles, then, in greater or lesser degree, are the causative factors in all success of whatsoever kind. Underneath all prosperity they are the strong supports, and, howsoever appearances may be against such a conclusion, a measure of them informs and sustains every effort which is crowned with that excellence which men name success.

It is true that comparatively few successful men practice, in their entirety and perfection, all these eight principles, but there are those who do, and they are the leaders, teachers, and guides of men, the supports of human society, and the strong pioneers in the van of human evolution.

But while few achieve that moral perfection which ensures the acme of success, all lesser successes come from the partial observance of these principles which are so powerful in the production of good results that even perfection in any two or three of them alone is sufficient to ensure an ordinary degree of prosperity, and maintain a measure of local influence at least for a time, while the same perfection in two or three with partial excellence in all, or nearly all, the others, will render permanent that limited success and influence which will, necessarily, grow and extend in exact ratio with a more intimate knowledge and practice of those principles which, at present, are only partially incorporated in the character.

The boundary lines of a man's morality mark the limits of his success. So true is this that to know a man's moral status would be to know—to gauge mathematically—his ultimate success or failure. The temple of prosperity only stands in so far as it is supported by its moral pillars; as they are weakened, it becomes insecure; in so far as they are withdrawn, it crumbles away and totters to ruin.

Ultimate failure and defeat are inevitable where moral principles are ignored or defied—inevitable in the nature of things as cause and effect. As a stone thrown upward returns to the earth, so every deed, good or bad, returns upon him that sent it forth. Every unmoral or immoral act frustrates the end at which it aims, and every such succeeding act puts it further and further away as an achieved realization. On the other hand, every moral act is another solid brick in the temple of prosperity, another round of strength and sculptured beauty in the pillars which support it.

Individuals, families, nations grow and prosper in harmony with their growth in moral strength and knowledge; they fall and fail in accordance with their moral decadence.

Mentally, as physically, only that which has form and solidity can stand and endure. The unmoral is nothingness, and from it nothing can be formed. It is the negation of substance. The immoral is destruction. It is the negation of form. It is a process of spiritual denudation. While it undermines and disintegrates, it leaves the scattered material ready for the wise builder to put it into form again; and the wise builder is *Morality*. The moral is substance, form, and building power in one. Morality always builds up and preserves, for that is its nature, being the opposite of immorality which always breaks down and destroys. Morality is the Master-builder everywhere, whether in individuals or nations, whether in the world or in the universe.

Morality is invincible, and he who stands upon it to the end, stands upon an impregnable rock, so that his defeat is impossible, his triumph certain. He will be tried, and that to the uttermost, for without fighting there can be no victory, and so only can his moral powers be perfected, and it is in the nature of fixed principles, as of everything finely and perfectly wrought, to have their strength tested and proved. The steel bars which are to perform the strongest and best uses in the world must be subjected to a severe strain by the ironmaster, as a test of their texture and efficiency, before they are sent from his foundry. The brick-maker throws aside the bricks which have given way under the severe heat. So he who is to be greatly and permanently successful will pass through the strain of adverse circumstances and the fire of temptation with his moral nature not merely not undermined, but strengthened and beautified. He will be like a bar of well-wrought steel, fit for the highest use, and the universe will see, as the ironmaster his finely-wrought steel, that the use does not escape him.

Immorality is assailable at every point, and he who tries to stand upon it, sinks into the morass of desolation. Even while his efforts seem to stand, they are crumbling away. The climax of failure is inevitable. While the immoral man is chuckling over his ill-gotten gains, there is already a hole in his pocket through which his gold is falling. While he who begins with morality, yet deserts it for gain in the hour of trial, is like the brick which breaks on the first application of heat; he is not fit for use, and the universe casts him aside: yet not finally, for he is a being, not a brick; and he can live and learn, can repent and be restored.

Moral force is the life of all success, and the sustaining element in all prosperity; but there are various kinds of success, and it is frequently necessary that a man should fail in one direction that he may reach up to a greater and more far-reaching success. If, for instance, a literary, artistic, or moral genius should begin by trying to make money, it may be, and often is, to his advantage and the betterment of his genius that he should fail therein, so that he may achieve that more sublime success wherein lies his real power. Many a millionaire would doubtless be willing to barter his millions for the literary successes of a Shakespeare or the spiritual success of a Buddha, and would thereby consider that he had made a good bargain. Exceptional moral success is rarely accompanied with riches, yet financial success cannot in any way compare with it in greatness and grandeur. But I am not, in this book, dealing with the success of the saint or moral genius (such being dealt with in other of my books), but with that success which concerns the welfare, well-being, and happiness of the broadly average man and woman,—in a word, with the prosperity of the mass of mankind; a success and prosperity which, while being more or less connected with money—being present and temporal—yet is not Confined thereto, but extends to and embraces all human activities, and which particularly relates to that harmony of the individual with his circumstances which produces that satisfaction called happiness and that comfort known as prosperity. To the achievement of this end, so desirable to the mass of mankind, let us now see how the eight principles operate, how the roof of prosperity is raised and made secure upon the pillars by which it is supported.

FIRST PILLAR
Energy

E nergy is the working power in all achievement. Inert coal it converts to fire, and water it transmutes into steam; it vivifies and intensifies the commonest talent until it approaches to genius, and when it touches the mind of the dullard, it turns into a living fire that which before was sleeping in inertia.

Energy is a moral virtue, its opposing vice being laziness. As a virtue, it can be cultivated, and the lazy man can become energetic by forcibly arousing himself to exertion. Compared with the energetic man, the lazy man is not half alive. Even while the latter is talking about the difficulty of doing a thing, the former is doing it. The active man has done a considerable amount of work before the lazy man has roused himself from sleep. While the lazy man is waiting for an opportunity, the active man has gone out, met and utilized half-a-dozen opportunities. He does things while the other is rubbing his eyes.

Energy is one of the primal forces; without it nothing can be accomplished. It is the basic element in all forms of action. The entire universe is a manifestation of tireless, though inscrutable energy. Energy is, indeed, life, and without it there would be no universe, no life. When a man has ceased to act, when the body lies inert, and all the functions have ceased to act, then we say he is dead; and in so far as a man fails to act, he is so far dead. Man, mentally and physically, is framed for action, and not for swinish ease. Every muscle of the body (being a lever for exertion) is a rebuke to the lazy man. Every bone and nerve is fashioned for resistance; every function and faculty is there for a legitimate use. All things have their end in action; all things are perfected in use.

This being so, there is no prosperity for the lazy man, no happiness, no refuge, and no rest; for him, there is not even the ease which he covets, for he at last becomes a homeless outcast, a troubled, harried, despised man, so that the proverb wisely puts it that, "The lazy man does the hardest work," in that, avoiding the systematic labour of skill, he brings upon himself the hardest lot.

The man of energy exerts himself to the accomplishment of some end, or ends. The end may be a good one or a bad one; but if a bad one, that is the abuse of energy which reacts destructively on the doer, like one striking a wall with his fist, and only injures his own hand. Energy is always good, but it is only useful when applied to good ends, and those ends, when reached, constitute happiness, success, prosperity.

Yet energy misapplied is better than no energy at all. This is powerfully put by St. John in the words: "I would have you either hot or cold; if you are lukewarm I will spew you out of my mouth." The extremes of heat and cold here symbolize the transforming agency of energy, in its good and bad aspects. The lukewarm stage is colourless, lifeless, useless; it can scarcely be said to have either virtue or vice, and is merely barren, empty, fruitless. The man who applies his abounding energy to bad ends, has, at least, one saving virtue, the virtue of exertion, and the very power with which he strives to acquire his selfish ends, will bring upon him such difficulties, pains, and sorrows, that will compel him to learn by experience, and so at last to refashion his base of action. At the right moment, when his mental eyes open to better purposes, he will turn round and cut new and proper channels for the outflow of his power, and will then be just as strong in good as he formerly was in evil. This truth is beautifully crystallized in the old proverb, "The greater the sinner, the greater the saint."

Energy is power, and without it there will be no accomplishment; there will not even be virtue, for virtue does not only consist of not doing evil, but also, and primarily, of doing good. There are those who try, yet fail through insufficient energy. Their efforts are too feeble to produce positive results. Such are not vicious, and because they never do any deliberate harm, are usually spoken of as good men that fail. But to lack the initiative to do harm is not to be good; it is only to be weak and powerless. He is the truly good man who, having the power to do evil, yet chooses to direct his energies in ways that are good. Without a considerable degree of energy, therefore, there will be no moral power. What good there is, will be latent and sleeping; there will be no going forth of good, just as there can be no mechanical motion without the motive power.

Energy is the informing power in all doing in every department of life, and whether it be along material or spiritual lines. The call to action which comes not only from the soldier but from the lips or pen of every teacher in every grade of thought, is a call to men to rouse their sleeping energy, and to do vigorously the task in hand. Even the men of contemplation and meditation never cease to rouse their disciples to exertion in meditative thought. Energy is alike needed in all spheres of life, and not only are the rules of the soldier, the engineer and the merchant rules of action, but nearly all the precepts of the saviours, sages, and saints are precepts of *doing.*

The advice of one of the Great Teachers to his disciples, "Keep wide awake," tersely expresses the necessity for tireless energy if one's purpose is to be accomplished, and is equally good advice to the salesman as to the saint. "Eternal vigilance is the price of liberty," and liberty is the reaching of one's fixed end. It was the same Teacher who said: "If anything is to be done, let a man do it at once; let him attack it vigorously!" The wisdom of this advice is seen when it is remembered that action is creative, that increase and development follow upon legitimate use. To get more energy we must use to the full that which we already possess. Only to him that hath is given. Only to him that puts his hand vigorously to some task do power and freedom come.

But energy to be productive must not only be directed toward good ends, it must be carefully controlled and conserved. "The conservation of energy" is a modern term expressive of that principle in nature by which no energy is wasted or

lost, and the man whose energies are to be fruitful in results must work intelligently upon this
principle. Noise and hurry are so much energy
running to waste. "More haste, less speed." The
maximum of noise usually accompanies the mini-
mum of accomplishment. With much talk there is
little doing. Working steam is not heard. It is the
escaping steam which makes a great noise. It is the
concentrated powder which drives the bullet to its
mark.

In so far as a man intensifies his energies by
conserving them and concentrating them upon
the accomplishment of his purpose, just so far does
he gain in quietness and silence, in repose and
calmness. It is a great delusion that noise means
power. There is no greater baby than the bluster-
ing boaster. Physically a man, he is but an infant
mentally, and having no strength to do anything,
and no work to show, he tries to make up for it by
loudly proclaiming what he has done, or could do.

"Still waters run deep," and the great universal forces are inaudible. Where calmness is, there
is the greatest power. Calmness is the sure indication of a strong, well-trained, patiently disciplined
mind. The calm man knows his business, be sure
of it. His words are few, but they tell. His schemes
are well planned, and they work true, like a well-
balanced machine. He sees a long way ahead, and

makes straight for his object. The enemy, Difficulty, he converts into a friend, and makes profitable use of him, for he has studied well how to "agree with his adversary while he is in the way with him." Like a wise general, he has anticipated all emergencies. Indeed, he is *the man who is prepared beforehand*. In his meditations, in the counsels of his judgment, he has conferred with causes, and has caught the bent of all contingencies. He is never taken by surprise; is never in a hurry, is safe in the keeping of his own steadfastness, and is sure of his ground. You may think you have got him, only to find, the next moment, that you have tripped in your haste, and that he has got you; or rather that you, wanting calmness, have hurried yourself into the dilemma which you had prepared for him. Your impulse cannot do battle with his deliberation, but is foiled at the first attack; your uncurbed energy cannot turn aside the wisely directed stream of his concentrated power. He is "armed at all points." By a mental Jiu-Jitsu acquired through self-discipline, he meets opposition in such a way that it destroys itself. Upbraid him with angry words, and the reproof hidden in his gentle reply searches to the very heart of your folly, and the fire of your anger sinks into the ashes of remorse. Approach him with a vulgar familiarity, and his look at once fills you with shame, and brings you back to your senses.

As he is prepared for all events, so he is ready for all men; though no men are ready for him. All weaknesses are betrayed in his presence, and he commands by an inherent force which calmness has rendered habitual and unconscious.

Calmness, as distinguished from the dead placidity of languor, is the acme of concentrated energy. There is a focused mentality behind it. In agitation and excitement the mentality is dispersed. It is irresponsible, and is without force or weight. The fussy, peevish, irritable man has no influence. He repels, and not attracts. He wonders why his "easy-going" neighbour succeeds, and is sought after, while he, who is always hurrying, worrying, and troubling (he miscalls it *striving*), fails, and is avoided. His neighbour, being a calmer man, not more easy-going but more deliberate, gets through more work, does it more skilfully, and is more self-possessed and manly. This is the reason of his success and influence. His energy is controlled and used, while the other man's energy is dispersed and abused.

Energy, then, is the first pillar in the temple of prosperity, and without it, as the first and most essential equipment, there can be no prosperity. No energy means no capacity; there is no aptitude for work, and therefore no manly self-respect and independence. Amongst the unemployed will be found many who are unemployable through sheer lack of this first essential of work—energy. The man that stands many hours a day at a street corner with his hands in his pockets and a pipe in his mouth, waiting for someone to treat him to a glass of beer, is little likely to find employment, or to accept it should it come to him. Physically flabby and mentally inert, he is every day becoming more so, is making himself more unfit to work, and therefore unfit to live. The energetic man may pass through temporary periods of unemployment and suffering, but it is impossible for him to become one of the permanently unemployed. He will either find work or make it, for inertia is painful to him, and work is a delight; and he who delights in work will not long remain unemployed.

The lazy man does not wish to be employed. He is in his element when doing nothing. His chief study is how to avoid exertion. To vegetate in semi-torpor is his idea of happiness. He is unfit and unemployable. Even the extreme Socialist, who places all unemployment at the door of the rich, would discharge a lazy servant, and so add one more to the army of the unemployed; for laziness is one of the lowest vices, repulsive to all active, right-minded men.

But energy is a composite power. It does not stand alone. Involved in it are qualities which go to the making of vigorous character and the production of prosperity. Mainly, these qualities are contained in the four following characteristics:

1. Promptitude.
2. Vigilance.
3. Industry.
4. Earnestness.

The pillar of energy is therefore a concrete mass composed of these four tenacious elements. They are tough, enduring, and are calculated to withstand the wildest weather of adversity. They all make for life, power, capacity, and progress.

✦ Promptitude ✦

Promptitude is a valuable possession. It begets reliability. People who are alert, prompt, and punctual are relied upon. They can be trusted to do their duty, and to do it vigorously and well. Masters who are prompt are a tonic to their employees, and a whip to those who are inclined to shirk. They are a means of wholesome discipline to those who would not otherwise discipline themselves. Thus while aiding their own usefulness and success, they contribute to the usefulness and success of others. The perfunctory worker, who is ever procrastinating, and is always behind time, becomes a nuisance, if not to himself, to others, and his services come to be regarded as of little economic value. Deliberation and despatch, handmaids of promptitude, are valuable aids in the achievement of prosperity. In ordinary business channels, alacrity is a saving power, and promptness spells profit.

It is doubtful whether a confirmed procrastinator ever succeeded in business. I have not yet met one such, though I have known many who have failed.

✦ Vigilance ✦

Vigilance is the guard of all the faculties and powers of the mind. It is the detective that prevents the entrance of any violent and destructive element. It is the close companion and protector of all success, liberty, and wisdom. Without this watchful attitude of mind, a man is a fool, and there is no prosperity for a fool. The fool allows his mind to be ransacked and robbed of its gravity, serenity, and judgment, by mean thoughts and violent passions as they come along to molest him. He is never on his guard, but leaves open the doors of his mind to every nefarious intruder. He is so weak and unsteady as to be swept off his balance by every gust of impulse that overtakes him. He is an example to others of what they should not be. He is always a failure, for the fool is an offence to all men, and there is no society that can receive him with respect. As wisdom is the acme of strength, so folly is the other extreme of weakness.

The lack of vigilance is shown in thoughtlessness, and in a general looseness in the common details of life. Thoughtlessness is but another name for folly. It lies at the root of a great deal of failure and misery. No one who aims at any kind of usefulness and prosperity (for usefulness in the body politic and prosperity to oneself cannot be severed), can afford to be asleep with regard to his actions and the effect of those actions on others and reactively on himself. He must, at the outset of his career, wake up to a sense of his personal responsibility. He must know that wherever he is—in the home, the counting-house, the pulpit, the store, in the schoolroom or behind the counter, in company or alone, at work or at play—his conduct will materially affect his career for good or bad; for there is a subtle influence in behaviour which leaves its impress on every man, woman, and child that it touches, and that impress is the determining factor in the attitude of persons toward one another. It is for this reason that the cultivation of good manners plays such an important part in all coherent society. If you carry about with you a disturbing or disagreeable mental defect, it needs not to be named and known to work its poison upon your affairs. Its corrosive influence will eat into all your efforts, and disfigure your happiness and prosperity, as a powerful acid eats into and disfigures the finest steel. On the other hand, if you carry about an assuring and harmonious mental excellence, it needs not that those about you understand it, to be influenced by it. They will be drawn toward you in good-will, often without knowing why, and that good quality will be the most powerful support in all your affairs, bringing you friends and opportunities, and greatly aiding in the success of all your enterprises. It will even right your mistakes, and largely neutralize the bad effects of your minor incapacities, covering a multitude of faults.

Thus we receive at the hands of the world according to the measure of our giving. For bad, bad; for good, good. For defective conduct, indifferent influence and imperfect success; for superior conduct, lasting power and consummate achievement. We act, and the world responds. When the foolish man fails, he blames others, and sees no error in himself; but the wise man watches and corrects himself, and so is assured of success.

The man whose mind is vigilant and alert, has thereby a valuable equipment in the achievement of his aims; and if he be fully alive and wide awake on all occasions, to all opportunities, and against all marring defects of character, what event, what circumstance, what enemy shall overtake him and find him unprepared? What shall prevent him from achieving the legitimate end at which he aims?

✦ Industry ✦

Industry brings cheerfulness and plenty. Vigorously industrious people are the happiest members of the community. They are not always the richest, if by riches is meant a superfluity of money; but they are always the most light-hearted and joyful, and the most satisfied with what they do and have, and are therefore the richer, if by richer we mean more abundantly blessed. Active people have no time for moping and brooding, or for dwelling selfishly upon their ailments and troubles.

Things most used are kept the brightest, and people most employed best retain their brightness and buoyancy of spirit. Things unused tarnish quickest; and the time-killer is attacked with ennui and morbid fancies. To talk of having to "kill time" is almost like a confession of imbecility; for who, in the short life at his disposal, and in a world so flooded with resources of knowledge and usefulness, can have too much time? People with sound heads and good hearts can fill up every moment of every day usefully and happily, and if they refer to time at all, it is to the effect that it is all too short to enable them to do all that they would like to do.

Industry, too, promotes health and well-being. The active man goes to bed tired every night; his rest is sound and sweet, and he wakes up early in the morning, fresh and strong for another day's delightful toil. His appetite and digestion are good. He has an excellent sauce in recreation, and a good tonic in toil. What companionship can such a man have with moping and melancholy? Such morbid spirits hang around those who do little and dine excessively. People who make themselves useful to the community, receive back from the community their full share of health, happiness, and prosperity. They brighten the daily task, and keep the world moving. They are the gold of the nation and the salt of the earth.

✦ Earnestness ✦

"Earnestness," said a Great Teacher, "is the path of immortality. They who are in earnest do not die; they who are not in earnest are as if dead already." Earnestness is the dedication of the entire mind to its task. We live only in what we do. Earnest people are dissatisfied with anything short of the highest excellence in whatever they do, and they always reach that excellence. There are so many that are careless and half-hearted, so satisfied with a poor performance, that the earnest ones shine apart, as it were, in their excellence. There are always plenty of "vacancies" in the ranks of usefulness and service for earnest people. There never was, and never will be, a deeply earnest man or woman who did not fill successfully some suitable sphere. Such people are scrupulous, conscientious, and painstaking, and cannot rest in ease until the very best is done, and the whole world is always on the lookout to reward the best. It always stands ready to pay the full price, whether in money, fame, friends, influence, happiness, scope, or life, for that which is of surpassing excellence, whether it be in things material, intellectual, or spiritual. Whatever you are,—whether shopkeeper or saintly teacher,—you can safely give the very best to the world without any doubt or misgiving. If the indelible impress of your earnestness be on your goods in one case, or on your words in the other, your business will flourish, or your precepts will live.

Earnest people make rapid progress both in their work and their character. It is thus that they live, and "do not die," for stagnation only is death, and where there is incessant progress and ever-ascending excellence, stagnation and death are swallowed up in activity and life.

Thus are the making and masonry of the First Pillar explained. He who builds it well, and sets it firm and straight, will have a powerful and enduring support in the business of his life.

SECOND PILLAR
Economy

I t is said of Nature that she knows no vacuum. She also knows no waste. In the divine economy of Nature everything is conserved and turned to good account. Even excreta are chemically transmuted, and utilized in the building up of new forms. Nature destroys every foulness, not by annihilation, but by transmutation, by sweetening and purifying it, and making it serve the ends of things beautiful, useful, and good.

That economy which, in nature, is a universal principle, is in man a moral quality, and it is that quality by which he preserves his energies, and sustains his place as a working unit in the scheme of things.

Financial economy is merely a fragment of this principle, or rather it is a material symbol of that true economy which is purely mental, and its transmutations spiritual. The financial economist exchanges coppers for silver, silver for gold, gold for notes, and the notes he converts into the figures of a bank account. By these conversions of money into more readily transmissible forms he is the gainer in the financial management of his affairs. The spiritual economist transmutes passions into intelligence, intelligence into principles, principles into wisdom, and wisdom is manifested in actions which are few but of powerful effect. By all these transmutations he is the gainer in character, and in the management of his life.

True economy is the middle way in all things, whether material or mental, between waste and undue retention. That which is wasted, whether money or mental energy, is rendered powerless; that which is selfishly retained and hoarded up, is equally powerless. To secure power, whether of capital or mentality, there must be concentration, but concentration must be followed by legitimate use. The gathering up of money or energy is only a means; the end is *use*; and it is use only that produces power.

An all-round economy consists in finding the middle way in the following seven things: *Money*, *Food*, *Clothing*, *Recreation*, *Rest*, *Time*, and *Energy*.

MONEY

Money is the symbol of exchange, and represents purchasing power. He who is anxious to acquire financial wealth—as well as he who wishes to avoid debt—must study how to apportion his expenditure in accordance with his income, so as to leave a margin of ever-increasing working capital, or to have a little store ready in hand for any emergency. Money spent in thoughtless expenditure—in worthless pleasures or harmful luxuries—is money wasted and power destroyed; for, although a limited and subordinate power, the means and capacity for legitimate and virtuous purchase is, nevertheless, a power, and one that enters largely into the details of our everyday life. The spendthrift can never become rich, but, if he begin with riches, must soon become poor. The miser, with all his stored-away gold, cannot be said to be rich, for he is in want, and his gold, lying idle, is deprived of its power of purchase. The thrifty and prudent are on the way to riches, for while they spend wisely they save carefully, and gradually enlarge their sphere as their growing means allow.

The poor man who is to become rich must begin at the bottom, and must not wish, nor try, to appear affluent by attempting something far beyond his means. There is always plenty of room and scope at the bottom, and it is a safe place from which to begin, as there is nothing below, and everything above. Many a young business man comes at once to grief by swagger and display which he foolishly imagines are necessary to success, but which, deceiving no one but himself, lead quickly to ruin. A modest and true beginning, in any sphere, will better ensure success than an exaggerated advertisement of one's standing and importance. The smaller the capital, the smaller should be the sphere of operations. Capital and scope are hand and glove, and they should fit. Concentrate your capital within the circle of its working power, and, however circumscribed that circle may be, it will continue to widen and extend as the gathering momentum of power presses for expression.

Above all, take care always to avoid the two extremes of parsimony and prodigality.

FOOD

Food represents life, vitality, and both physical and mental strength. There is a middle way in eating and drinking, as in all else. The man who is to achieve prosperity must be well nourished, but not overfed. The man that starves his body, whether through miserliness or asceticism (both forms of false economy), diminishes his mental energy, and renders his body too enfeebled to be the instrument for any strong achievement. Such a man courts sickly-mindedness, a condition conducive only to failure.

The glutton, however, destroys himself by excess. His bestialized body becomes a stored-up reservoir of poisons which attract disease and corruption, while his mind becomes more and more brutalized and confused, and therefore more incapable. Gluttony is one of the lowest and most animal vices, and is obnoxious to all who pursue a moderate course.

The best workers and most successful men are they who are most moderate in eating and drinking. By taking enough nourishment, but not too much, they attain the maximum physical and mental fitness. Being thus well equipped by moderation, they are enabled vigorously and joyfully to fight the battle of life.

CLOTHING

Clothing is covering and protection for the body; though it is frequently wrested from this economic purpose, and made a means of vain display. The two extremes to be avoided here are negligence and vanity. Custom cannot, and need not, be ignored; and cleanliness is all-important. The ill-dressed, unkempt man or woman invites failure and loneliness. A man's dress should harmonize with his station in life, and it should be of good quality, and be well-made and appropriate. Clothing should not be cast aside while comparatively new, but should be well worn. If a man be poor, he will not lose in either self-respect or the respect of others by wearing threadbare clothing, if it be clean, and his whole body be clean and neat. But vanity, leading to excessive luxury in clothing, is a vice which should be studiously avoided by virtuous people. I knew a lady who had forty dresses in her wardrobe; also a man who had twenty walking-sticks, about the same number of hats, and some dozen mackintoshes; while another had some twenty or thirty pairs of boots. Rich people who thus squander money on piles of superfluous clothing, are courting poverty; for it is waste, and waste leads to want. The money so heedlessly spent could be better used, for suffering abounds and charity is noble.

An obtrusive display in clothing and jewellery bespeaks a vulgar and empty mind. Modest and cultured people are modest and becoming in their dress, and their spare money is wisely used in further enhancing their culture and virtue. Education and progress are of more importance to them than vain and needless apparel; and literature, art, and science are encouraged thereby. A true refinement is in the mind and behaviour, and a mind adorned with virtue and intelligence cannot add to its attractiveness (though it may detract from it) by an ostentatious display of the body. Time spent in uselessly adorning the body could be more fruitfully employed. Simplicity in dress, as in other things, is the best. It touches the point of excellence in usefulness, comfort, and bodily grace, and bespeaks true taste and cultivated refinement.

RECREATION

Recreation is one of the necessities of life. Every man and woman should have some definite work as the main object of life, and to which a considerable amount of time should be devoted, and he should only turn from it at given and limited periods for recreation and rest. The object of recreation is greater buoyancy of both body and mind, with an increase of power in one's serious work. It is, therefore, a means, not an end; and this should ever be borne in mind, for, to many, some forms of recreation—innocent and good in themselves—become so fascinating, that they are in danger of making them the end of life, and of thus abandoning duty for pleasure. To make of life a ceaseless round of games and pleasures, with no other object in life, is to turn living upside-down, as it were, and it produces monotony and enervation. People who do it are the most unhappy of mortals, and suffer from languor, ennui, and peevishness. As sauce is an aid to digestion, and can only produce sickness if taken as food, so recreation is a refreshment in the intervals of labour, and can only lead to misery when made the work of life. When a man has done his day's duty he can turn to his recreation with a freed mind and a light heart, and both his work and his pleasure will be to him a source of happiness.

It is a true economy in this particular neither to devote the whole of one's time to work nor to recreation, but to apportion to each its time and place; and so fill out life with those changes which are necessary to a long life and a fruitful existence.

All agreeable change is recreation, and the mental worker will gain both in the quality and quantity of his work by laying it down at the time appointed for restful and refreshing recreation; while the physical worker will improve in every way by turning to some form of study as a hobby or means of education.

As we do not spend all our time in eating, or sleeping, or resting, neither should we spend it in exercise or pleasure, but should give recreation its proper place as a natural tonic in the economic scheme of our life.

REST

Rest is for recuperation after toil. Every self-respecting human being should do sufficient work every day to make his sleep restful and sweet, and his rising up fresh and bright.

Enough sleep should be taken, but not too much. Over-indulgence on the one hand, or deprivation on the other, are both harmful. It is an easy matter to find out how much sleep one requires. By going to bed early, and getting up early (rising a little earlier every morning if one has been in the habit of spending long hours in bed), one can very soon accurately gauge and adjust the number of hours he or she requires for complete recuperation. It will be found as the sleeping hours are shortened that the sleep becomes more and more sound and sweet, and the waking up more and more alert and bright. People who are to prosper in their work must not give way to ignoble ease and over-indulgence in sleep. Fruitful labour, and not ease, is the true end of life, and ease is only good in so far as it subserves the ends of work. Sloth and prosperity can never be companions, can never even approach each other. The sluggard will never overtake success, but failure will speedily catch up with him, and leave him defeated. Rest is to fit us for greater labour, and not to pamper us in indolence. When the bodily vigour is restored, the end of rest is accomplished. A perfect balance between labour and rest contributes considerably to health, happiness, and prosperity.

TIME

Time is that which we all possess in equal measure. The day is not lengthened for any man. We should therefore see to it that we do not squander its precious minutes in unprofitable waste. He who spends his time in self-indulgence and the pursuit of pleasure, presently finds himself old, and nothing has been accomplished. He who fills full with useful pursuits the minutes as they come and go, grows old in honour and wisdom, and prosperity abides with him. Money wasted can be restored; health wasted can be restored; but time wasted can never be restored.

It is an old saying that "time is money." It is, in the same way, health, and strength, and talent, and genius, and wisdom, in accordance with the manner in which it is used; and to properly use it, the minutes must be seized upon as they come, for once they are past they can never be recalled. The day should be divided into portions, and everything—work, leisure, meals, recreation— should be attended to in its proper time; and the time of *preparation* should not be overlooked or ignored. Whatever a man does, he will do it better

and more successfully by utilizing some small portion of the day in preparing his mind for his work.
The man who gets up early in order to think and
plan, that he may weigh and consider and forecast,
will always manifest greater skill and success in
his particular pursuit than the man who lies in
bed till the last moment, and only gets up just in
time to begin breakfast. An hour spent in this way
before breakfast will prove of the greatest value
in making one's efforts fruitful. It is a means of
calming and clarifying the mind, and of focussing
one's energies so as to render them more powerful
and effective. The best and most abiding success
is that which is made before eight o'clock in the
morning. He who is at his business at six o'clock,
will always—all other conditions being equal—be
a long way ahead of the man who is in bed at eight.
The lie-a-bed heavily handicaps himself in the race
of life. He gives his early-rising competitor two or
three hours' start every day. How can he ever hope
to win with such a self-imposed tax upon his time?
At the end of a year that two or three hours' start
every day is shown in a success which is the syn-
thesis of accumulated results. What, then, must
be the difference between the efforts of these two
men at the end, say, of twenty years! The lie-a-bed,
too, after he gets up is always in a hurry trying
to regain lost time, which results in more loss of

time, for hurry always defeats its own end. The early riser, who thus economizes his time, has no need to hurry, for he is always ahead of the hour, is always well up with his work; he can well afford to be calm and deliberate, and to do carefully and well whatever is in hand, for his good habit shows itself at the end of the day in the form of a happy frame of mind, and in bigger results in the shape of work skilfully and successfully done.

In the economizing of time, too, there will be many things which a man will have to eliminate from his life; some of the things and pursuits which he loves, and desires to retain, will have to be sacrificed to the main purpose of his life. The studied elimination of non-essentials from one's daily life is a vital factor in all great achievement. All great men are adepts in this branch of economy, and it plays an important part in the making of their greatness. It is a form of economy which also enters into the mind, the actions, and the speech, eliminating from them all that is superfluous, and that impedes, and does not subserve, the end aimed at. Foolish and unsuccessful people talk carelessly and aimlessly, act carelessly and aimlessly, and allow everything that comes along— good, bad, and indifferent—to lodge in their mind. The mind of the true economist is a sieve which lets everything fall through except that which is of use to him in the business of his life. He also employs only necessary words, and does only necessary actions, thus vastly minimizing friction and waste of power.

To go to bed betime and to get up betime, to fill in every working minute with purposeful thought and effective action, this is the true economy of time.

ENERGY

Energy is economized by the formation of good habits. All vices are a reckless expenditure of energy. Sufficient energy is thoughtlessly wasted in bad habits to enable men to accomplish the greatest success, if conserved and used in right directions. If economy be practised in the six points already considered, much will be done in the conservation of one's energies; but a man must go still further, and carefully husband his vitality by the avoidance of all forms of vice; and by vice is meant not only all forms of physical self-indulgences and impurities, but also all those mental vices such as hurry, worry, excitement, despondency, anger, complaining and envy—which deplete the mind and render it unfit for any important work or admirable achievement. They are common forms of mental dissipation which a man of character should study how to avoid and overcome. The energy wasted in frequent fits of bad temper would, if controlled and properly directed, give a man strength of mind, force of character, and much power to achieve. The angry man is a strong man made weak by the dissipation of his mental energy. He needs self-control to manifest his strength. The calm man is always his superior in any department of life, and will always take precedence of him, both in his success, and in the estimation of others. No man can afford to disperse his energies in fostering bad habits and bad tendencies of mind. Every vice, however apparently small, will tell against him in the battle of life. Every harmful self-indulgence will come back to him in the form of some trouble or weakness. Every moment of riot or of pandering to his lower inclinations will make his progress more laborious, and will hold him back from scaling the high heaven of his wished-for achievement. On the other hand, he who economizes his energies, and bends them toward the main task of his life, will make rapid progress, and nothing will prevent him from reaching the golden city of success.

It will be seen that economy is something far more profound and far-reaching than the mere saving of money. It touches every part of our nature and every phase of our life. The old saying, "Take care of the pence, and the pounds will take care of themselves," may be regarded as a parable, for the lower passions of men are not bad of themselves when regarded as native energy; it is the abuse of that energy that is bad, and if this passional energy be taken care of and stored up and transmuted, it reappears as force of character. To waste this valuable energy in the pursuit of vice is like wasting the pence, and so losing the pounds; but to take care of it for good uses is to store up the pence of passions, and so gain the golden pounds of good. Take care, therefore, of the lower energies, and the higher achievements will take care of themselves.

The Pillar of Economy, when soundly built, will be found to be composed largely of these four qualities:

1. Moderation.
2. Efficiency.
3. Resourcefulness.
4. Originality.

✦ Moderation ✦

Moderation is the strong core of economy. It avoids extremes, finding the middle way in all things. It also consists in abstaining from the unnecessary and the harmful. There can be no such thing as moderation in that which is evil, for that would be excess. A true moderation abstains from evil. It is not a moderate use of fire to put our hands into it, but to warm them by it at a safe distance. Evil is a fire that will burn a man though he but touch it. A harmful luxury is best left severely alone. Smoking, snuff-taking, alcoholic drinking, gambling, and other such common vices, although they have dragged thousands down to ill-health, misery, and failure, have never helped one toward health, happiness, and success. The man who eschews them will always be ahead of the man that pursues them, their talents and opportunities being equal. Healthy, happy, and long-lived people are always moderate and abstemious in their habits. By moderation the life-forces are preserved; by excess they are destroyed. Men, also, who carry moderation into their thoughts, allaying their passions and feelings, avoiding all unwholesome extremes and morbid sensations and sentiments, add knowledge and wisdom to happiness and health, and thereby attain to the highest felicity and power. The immoderate destroy themselves by their own folly. They weaken their energies and stultify their capabilities, and instead of achieving an abiding success, reach only, at best, a fitful and precarious prosperity.

✦ Efficiency ✦

Efficiency proceeds from the right conservation of one's forces and powers. All skill is the use of concentrated energy. Superior skill, as talent and genius, is a higher degree of concentrated force. Men are always skillful in that which they love, because the mind is almost ceaselessly centred upon it. Skill is the result of that mental economy which transmutes thought into invention and action. There will be no prosperity without skill, and one's prosperity will be in the measure of one's skill. By a process of natural selection, the inefficient fall into their right places among the badly paid or unemployed; for who will employ a man who cannot, or will not, do his work properly? An employer may occasionally keep such a man out of charity; but this will be exceptional, as places of business, offices, households, and all centres of organized activity, are not charitable institutions, but industrial bodies which stand or fall by the fitness and efficiency of their individual members. Skill is gained by thoughtfulness and attention. Aimless and inattentive people are usually out of employment, to wit, the lounger at the street corner. They cannot do the simplest thing properly, because they will not rouse up the mind to thought and attention. Recently an acquaintance of mine employed a tramp to clean his windows, but the man had refrained from work and systematic thought for so long that he had become incapable of both, and could not even clean a window. Even when shown how to do it, he could not follow the simple instructions given. This is an instance, too, of the fact that the simplest thing requires a measure of skill in the doing. Efficiency largely determines a man's place among his fellows, and leads one on by steps to higher and higher positions as greater powers are developed. The good workman is skillful with his tools, while the good man is skillful with his thoughts. Wisdom is the highest form of skill. Aptitude is incipient wisdom. There is *one* right way of doing everything, even the smallest, and a thousand wrong ways. Skill consists in finding the one right way, and adhering to it. The inefficient bungle confusedly about among the thousand wrong ways, and do not adopt the right even when it is pointed out to them. They do this in some cases because they think, in their ignorance, that they know best, thereby placing themselves in a position where it becomes impossible to learn, even though it be only to learn how to clean a window or sweep a floor. Thoughtlessness and inefficiency are all too common. There is plenty of room in the world for thoughtful and efficient people. Employers of labour know how difficult it is to get the best workmanship. The good workman, whether with tools or brain, whether with speech or thought, will always find a place for the exercise of his skill.

✦ Resourcefulness ✦

Resourcefulness is the outcome of efficiency. It is an important element in prosperity, for the resourceful man is never confounded. He may have many falls, but he will always be equal to the occasion, and will be on his feet again immediately. Resourcefulness has its fundamental cause in the conservation of energy. It is energy transmuted. When a man cuts off certain mental or bodily vices which have been depleting him of his energy, what becomes of the energy so conserved? It is not destroyed or lost, for energy can never be destroyed or lost. *It becomes productive energy.* It reappears in the form of fruitful thought. The virtuous man is always more successful than the vicious man because he is teeming with resources. His entire mentality is alive and vigorous, abounding with stored-up energy. What the vicious man wastes in vicious indulgence, the virtuous man uses in fruitful industry. A new life and a new world, abounding with all fascinating pursuits and pure delights, opens up to the man who shuts himself off from the old world of animal vice, and his place will be assured by the resources which will well up within him. Barren seed perishes in the earth; there is no place for it in the fruitful economy of nature. Barren minds sink in the struggle of life. Human society makes for good, and there is no room in it for the emptiness engendered by vice. But the barren mind will not sink forever. When it wills, it can become fruitful, and regain itself. By the very nature of existence, by the eternal law of progress, the vicious man *must* fall; but having fallen, he can rise again. He can turn from vice to virtue, and stand, self-respecting and secure, upon his own resources.

The resourceful men invent, discover, initiate. They cannot fail, for they are in the stream of progress. They are full of new schemes, new methods, new hopes, and their life is so much fuller and richer thereby. They are men of supple minds. When a man fails to improve his business, his work, his methods, he falls out of the line of progress, and has begun to fail. His mind has become stiff and inert like the body of an aged man, and so fails to keep pace with the rapidly moving ideas and plans of resourceful minds. A resourceful mind is like a river which never runs dry, and which affords refreshment, and supplies new vigour in times of drought. Men of resources are men of new ideas, and men of new ideas flourish where others fade and decay.

✦ Originality ✦

Originality is resourcefulness ripened and perfected. Where there is originality there is genius, and men of genius are the lights of the world. Whatever work a man does, he should fall back upon his own resources in the doing it. While learning from others he should not slavishly imitate them, but should put himself into his work, and so make it new and original. Original men get the ear of the world. They may be neglected at first, but they are always ultimately accepted, and become patterns for mankind. Once a man has acquired the knack of originality, he takes his place as a leader among men in his particular department of knowledge and skill. But originality cannot be forced; it can only be developed; and it is developed by proceeding from excellence to excellence, by ascending in the scale of skill by the full and right use of one's mental powers. Let a man consecrate himself to his work, let him, so consecrated, concentrate all his energies upon it, and the day will come when the world will hail him as one of its strong sons; and he, too, like Balzac, who after many years of strenuous toil one day exclaimed, "I am about to become a genius!" will at last discover, to his joy, that he has joined the company of original minds, the gods who lead mankind into newer, higher, and more beneficent ways.

The composition of the Second Pillar is thus revealed. Its building awaits the ready workman who will skilfully apply his mental energies.

THIRD PILLAR
Integrity

There is no striking a cheap bargain with prosperity. It must be purchased, not only with intelligent labour, but with moral force. As the bubble cannot endure, so the fraud cannot prosper. He makes a feverish spurt in the acquirement of money, and then collapses. Nothing is ever gained, ever can be gained, by fraud. It is but wrested for a time, to be again returned with heavy interest. But fraud is not Confined to the unscrupulous swindler. All who are getting, or trying to get, money without giving an equivalent are practicing fraud, whether they know it or not. Men who are anxiously scheming how to get money without working for it, are frauds, and mentally they are closely allied to the thief and swindler under whose influence they come, sooner or later, and who deprives them of their capital. What is a thief but a man who carries to its logical extreme the desire to possess without giving a just return—that is, unlawfully? The man that courts prosperity must, in all his transactions, whether material or mental, study how to give a just return for that which he receives. This is the great fundamental principle in all sound commerce, while in spiritual things it becomes the doing to others that which we would have them do to us, and applied to the forces of the universe, it is scientifically stated in the formula, "Action and reaction are equal."

Human life is reciprocal, not rapacious, and the man who regards all others as his legitimate prey will soon find himself stranded in the desert of ruin, far away from the path of prosperity. He is too far behind in the process of evolution to cope successfully with honest men. The fittest, the best, always survive, and he, being the worst, cannot therefore continue. His end, unless he change in time, is sure—it is the jail, the filthy hovel, or the place of the deserted outcast. His efforts are destructive, and not constructive, and he thereby destroys himself.

It was Carlyle who, referring to Mohammed being then universally regarded by Christians as an impostor, exclaimed, "An impostor found a religion! An impostor couldn't build a brick house!" An

impostor, a liar, a cheat—the man of dishonesty—
cannot build, as he has neither tools nor material
with which to build. He can no more build up a
business, a character, a career, a success, than he
can found a religion or build a brick house. He not
only does not build, but all his energies are bent
on undermining what others have built, but this
being impossible, he undermines himself.

Without integrity, energy and economy will at
last fail, but aided by integrity, their strength will
be greatly augmented. There is not an occasion
in life in which the moral factor does not play an
important part. Sterling integrity tells wherever
it is, and stamps its hall-mark on all transactions;
and it does this because of its wonderful coherence
and consistency, and its invincible strength. For the
man of integrity is in line with the fixed laws of
things—not only with the fundamental principles
on which human society rests, but with the laws
which hold the vast universe together. Who shall
set these at naught? Who then shall undermine the
man of unblemished integrity? He is like a strong
tree whose roots are fed by perennial springs, and
which no tempest can lay low.

To be complete and strong, integrity must
embrace the whole man, and extend to all the
details of his life; and it must be so thorough and
permanent as to withstand all temptations to

swerve into compromise. To fail in one point is to fail in all, and to admit, under stress, a compromise with falsehood, howsoever necessary and insignificant it may appear, is to throw down the shield of integrity, and to stand exposed to the onslaughts of evil.

The man who works as carefully and conscientiously when his employer is away as when his eye is upon him, will not long remain in an inferior position. Such integrity in duty, in performing the details of his work, will quickly lead him into the fertile regions of prosperity.

The shirker, on the other hand, he who does not scruple to neglect his work when his employer is not about—thereby robbing his employer of the time and labour for which he is paid—will quickly come to the barren region of unemployment, and will look in vain for needful labour.

There will come a time, too, to the man who is not deeply rooted in integrity, when it will seem necessary to his prospects and prosperity that he should tell a lie or do a dishonest thing—I say, to the man who is not deeply rooted in this principle, for a man of fixed and enlightened integrity knows that lying and dishonesty can never under any circumstance be necessary, and therefore he neither needs to be tempted in this particular, nor can he possibly be tempted—but the one so tempted must be able to cast aside the subtle insinuation of false-hood which in a time of indecision and perplexity arises within him, and he must stand firmly by the principle, being willing to lose and suffer rather than sink into obliquity. In this way only can he become enlightened concerning this moral principle, and discover the glad truth that integrity does not lead to loss and suffering, but to gain and joy; that honesty and deprivation are not, and cannot be, related as cause and effect.

It is this willingness to sacrifice rather than be untrue that leads to enlightenment in all spheres of life; and the man who, rather than sacrifice some selfish aim, will lie or deceive, has forfeited his right to moral enlightenment, and takes his place lower down among the devotees of deceit, among the doers of shady transactions, and men of no character and no reputation.

A man is not truly armoured with integrity until he has become incapable of lying or deceiving either by gesture, word, or act; until he sees, clearly, openly, and freed from all doubt, the deadly effects of such moral turpitude. The man so enlightened is protected from all quarters, and can no more be undermined by dishonest men than the sun can be pulled down from heaven by madmen, and the arrows of selfishness and treachery that may be poured upon him will rebound from the strong armour of his integrity and the bright shield of his righteousness, leaving him unarmed and untouched.

A lying tradesman will tell you that no man can thrive and be honest in these days of keen competition. How can such a man know this, seeing that he has never tried honesty? Moreover, such a man has no knowledge of honesty, and his statement is, therefore, a statement of ignorance, and ignorance and falsehood so blind a man that he foolishly imagines all are as ignorant and false as himself. I have known such tradesmen, and have seen them come to ruin. I once heard a business man make the following statement in a public meeting: "No man can be entirely honest in business; he can only be approximately honest." He imagined that his statement revealed the condition of the business world; it did not; *it revealed his own condition*. He was merely telling his audience that he was a dishonest man, but his ignorance, moral ignorance, prevented him from seeing this. Approximate honesty is only another term for dishonesty. The man who deviates a little from the straight path, will deviate more. He has no fixed principle of right, and is only thinking of his own advantage. That he persuades himself that *his* particular dishonesty is of a white and harmless kind, and that he is not so bad as his neighbour, is only one of the many forms of self-delusion which ignorance of moral principles creates.

Right-doing between man and man in the varied relations and transactions of life is the very soul of integrity. It includes, but is more than, honesty. It is the backbone of human society, and the support of human institutions. Without it there would be no trust, no confidence between men, and the business world would topple to its fall.

As the liar thinks all men are liars, and treats them as such, so the man of integrity treats all men with confidence. He trusts them, and they trust him. His clear eye and open hand shame the creeping fraud so that he cannot practice his fraud on him. As Emerson has so finely put it: "Trust men and they will be true to you, even though they make an exception in your favour to all their rules of trade."

The upright man by his very presence commands the morality of those about him, making them better than they were. Men are powerfully influenced by one another, and, as good is more powerful than evil, the strong and good man both shames and elevates, by his contact, the weak and bad.

The man of integrity carries about with him an unconscious grandeur which both awes and inspires. Having lifted himself above the petty, the mean, and the false, these coward vices slink from his presence in confusion. The highest intellectual gift cannot compare with this lofty moral grandeur. In the memory of men and the estimation of the world the man of integrity occupies a higher place than the man of genius. Buckminster says, "The moral grandeur of an independent integrity is the sublimest thing in nature." It is the quality in man which produces heroes. The man of unswerving rectitude is intrinsically always a hero. It only needs the occasion to bring out the heroic element. He is always, too, possessed of a permanent happiness. The man of genius may be very unhappy, but not so the man of integrity. Nothing—nor sickness, nor calamity, nor death—can deprive him of that permanent satisfaction which inheres in uprightness.

Rectitude leads straight to prosperity by four successive steps. First, the upright man wins the confidence of others. Second, having gained their confidence, they put trust in him. Third, this trust, never being violated, produces a good reputation; and fourth, a good reputation spreads further and further, and so brings about success.

Dishonesty has the reverse effect. By destroying the confidence of others, it produces in them suspicion and mistrust, and these bring about a bad reputation which culminates in failure.

The Pillar of Integrity is held together by these four virile elements:

1. Honesty.
2. Fearlessness.
3. Purposefulness.
4. Invincibility.

✦ Honesty ✦

Honesty is the surest way to success. The day at last comes when the dishonest man repents in sorrow and suffering; but no man ever needs to repent of having been honest. Even when the honest man fails—as he does sometimes through lacking other of these pillars, such as energy, economy, or system—his failure is not the grievous thing it is to the dishonest man, for he can always rejoice in the fact that he has never defrauded a fellow-being. Even in his darkest hour he finds repose in a clear conscience.

Ignorant men imagine that dishonesty is a short cut to prosperity. This is why they practice it. The dishonest man is morally short-sighted. Like the drunkard who sees the immediate pleasure of his habit, but not the ultimate degradation, he sees the immediate effect of a dishonest act—a larger profit—but not its ultimate outcome; he does not see that an accumulated number of such acts must inevitably undermine his character, and bring his business toppling about his ears in ruin. While pocketing his gains, and thinking how cleverly and successfully he is imposing on others, he is all the time imposing on himself, and every coin thus gained *must* be paid back with added interest, and from this just retribution there is no possible loophole of escape. This moral gravitation is as sure and unvarying as the physical gravitation of a stone to the earth.

The tradesman who demands of his assistants that they shall lie, and misrepresent his goods to customers, is surrounding himself on all hands with suspicion, mistrust, and hatred. Even the moral weaklings who carry out his instructions despise him while defiling themselves with his unclean work. How can success thrive in such a poisonous atmosphere? The spirit of ruin is already in such a business, and the day of its fall is ordained.

An honest man may fail, but not because he is honest, and his failure will be honourable, and will not injure his character and reputation. His failure, too, resulting doubtless from his incapacity in the particular direction of his failure, will be a means of leading him into something more suited to his talents, and thus to ultimate success.

Fair dealing is admired by all; even the dishonest admire it in others, and he who deals justly with others in all his business transactions, who speaks the truth, and abides by his contracts even when they turn out to his own loss, such a man need fear no evil, for his actions can only result in good to himself and all with whom he is concerned.

✦ Fearlessness ✦

Fearlessness accompanies honesty. The honest man has a clear eye and an unflinching gaze. He looks his fellow-men in the face, and his speech is direct and convincing. The liar and cheat hangs his head; his eye is muddy and his gaze oblique. He cannot look another man in the eye, and his speech arouses mistrust, for it is ambiguous and unconvincing.

When a man has fulfilled his obligations, he has nothing to fear. All his business relations are safe and secure. His methods and actions will endure the light of day. Should he pass through a difficult time, and get into debt, everybody will trust him and be willing to wait for payment, and all his debts will be paid. Dishonest people try to avoid paying their debts, and they live in fear; but the honest man tries to avoid getting into debt, but when debt overtakes him, he does not fear, but, redoubling his exertions, his debts are paid.

The dishonest are always in fear. They do not fear debt, but fear that they will have to pay their debts. They fear their fellow-men, fear the established authorities, fear the results of all that they do, and they are in constant fear of their misdeeds being revealed, and the consequences which may at any moment overtake them.

The honest man is rid of all this burden of fear. He is light-hearted, and walks erect among his fellows; not assuming a part and skulking and cringing, but being himself, and meeting eye to eye. Not deceiving or injuring any, there are none to fear, and anything said against him can only redound to his advantage.

And this fearlessness is, in itself, a tower of strength in a man's life, supporting him through all emergencies, enabling him to battle manfully with difficulties, and in the end securing for him that success of which he cannot be dispossessed.

✦ Purposefulness ✦

Purposefulness is the direct outcome of that strength of character which integrity fosters. The man of integrity is the man of direct aims and strong and intelligent purposes. He does not guess, and work in the dark. All his plans have in them some of that moral fibre of which his character is wrought. A man's work will always in some way reflect himself, and the man of sound integrity is the man of sound plans. He weighs and considers and looks ahead, and so is less likely to make serious mistakes, or to bungle into a dilemma from which it is difficult to escape. Taking a moral view of all things, and always considering moral consequences, he stands on a firmer and more exalted ground than the man of mere policy and expedience; and while commanding a more extended view of any situation, he wields the greater power which a more comprehensive grasp of details, with the principles involved, confers upon him. Morality always has the advantage of expediency. Its purposes always reach down far below the surface, and are therefore more firm and secure, more strong and lasting. There is a native directness, too, about integrity, which enables the man to go straight to the mark in whatever he does, and which makes failure almost impossible.

Strong men have strong purposes, and strong purposes lead to strong achievements. The man of integrity is above all men *strong*, and his strength is manifested in that thoroughness with which he does the business of his life; a thoroughness which commands respect, admiration, and success.

✦ Invincibility ✦

Invincibility is a glorious protector, but it only envelopes the man whose integrity is perfectly pure and unassailable. Never to violate, even in the most insignificant particular, the principle of integrity, is to be invincible against all the assaults of innuendo, slander, and misrepresentation. The man who has failed in one point is vulnerable, and the shaft of evil, entering that point, will lay him low, like the arrow in the heel of Achilles. Pure and perfect integrity is proof against all attack and injury, enabling its possessor to meet all opposition and persecution with dauntless courage and sublime equanimity. No amount of talent, intellect, or business acumen can give a man that power of mind and peace of heart which come from an enlightened acceptance and observance of lofty moral principles. Moral force is the greatest power. Let the seeker for a true prosperity discover this force, let him foster and develop it in his mind and in his deeds, and as he succeeds he will take his place among the strong leaders of the earth.

Such is the strong and adamantine Pillar of Integrity. Blessed and prosperous above all men will be he who builds its incorruptible masonry into the temple of his life.

FOURTH PILLAR
System

System is that principle of order by which confusion is rendered impossible. In the natural and universal order everything is in its place, so that the vast universe runs more perfectly than the most perfect machine. Disorder in space would mean the destruction of the universe; and disorder in a man's affairs destroys his work and his prosperity.

All complex organizations are built up by system. No business or society can develop into large dimensions apart from system, and this principle is pre-eminently the instrument of the merchant, the business man, and the organizer of institutions.

There are many departments in which a disorderly man may succeed—although attention to order would increase his success—but he will not succeed in business, unless he can place the business entirely in the hands of a systematic manager, who will thereby remedy his own defect.

All large business concerns have been evolved along definitely drawn systematic lines, any violation of which would be disastrous to the efficiency and welfare of the business. Complex business or other organizations are built up like complex bodies in nature, by scrupulous attention to details. The disorderly man thinks he can be careless about everything but the main end, but by ignoring the means he frustrates the end. By the disarrangement of details, organisms perish, and by the careless neglect of details, the growth of any work or concern is prevented.

Disorderly people waste an enormous amount of time and energy. The time frittered away in hunting for things is sufficient, were it conserved by order, to enable them to achieve any success, for slovenly people never have a place for anything, and have to hunt, frequently for a long time, for any article which they require. In the irritation, bad humour, and chagrin which this daily hunting for things brings about, as much energy is dissipated as would be required to build up a big business, or scale the highest heights of achievement in any direction.

Orderly people conserve both their time and energy. They never lose anything, and therefore never have to find anything. Everything is in its place, and the hand can be at once placed upon it, though it be in the dark. They can well afford to be cool and deliberate, and so use their mental energies in something more profitable than irritation, bad temper, and accusing others for their own lack of order.

There is a kind of genius in system which can perform apparent wonders with ease. A systematic man can get through so great a quantity of work in such a short time, and with such freedom from exhaustion, as to appear almost miraculous. He scales the heights of success while his slovenly competitor is wallowing hopelessly in the bogs of confusion. His strict observance of the law of order enables him to reach his ends swiftly and smoothly, without friction or loss of time.

The demands of system, in all departments of the business world, are as rigid and exacting as the holy vows of a saint, and cannot be violated in the smallest particular but at the risk of one's financial prospects. In the financial world, the law of order is an iron necessity, and he who faultlessly observes it, saves time, temper, and money.

Every enduring achievement in human society rests upon a basis of system; so true is this, that were system withdrawn, progress would cease. Think, for instance, of the vast achievements of literature—the works of classic authors and of great geniuses; the great poems, the innumerable prose works, the monumental histories, the soul-stirring orations; think also of the social intercourse of human society, of its religions, its legal statutes, and its vast fund of book-knowledge—think of all these wonderful resources and achievements of language, and then reflect that they all depend for their origin, growth, and continuance on the systematic arrangement of twenty-six letters, an arrangement having inexhaustible and illimitable results by the fact of its rigid limitation within certain fixed rules.

Again, all the wonderful achievements of mathematics have come from the systematic arrangement of ten figures; while the most complex piece of machinery, with its thousands of parts working together smoothly and almost noiselessly to the achievement of the end for which it was designed, was brought forth by the systematic observance of a few mechanical laws.

Herein we see how system simplifies that which is complex; how it makes easy that which was difficult; how it relates an Infinite variety of details to the one central law of order, and so enables them to be dealt with and accounted for with perfect regularity, and with an entire absence of confusion.

The scientist names and classifies the myriad details of the universe, from the microscopic rotifer to the telescopic star, by his observance of the principle of system, so that out of many millions of objects, reference can be made to any one object in, at most, a few minutes. It is this faculty of speedy reference and swift dispatch which is of such overwhelming importance in every department of knowledge and industry, and the amount of time and labour thus saved to humanity is so vast as to be incomputable. We speak of religious, political, and business systems; of systems of thought, education, travel, government, and so on, indicating that all things in human society are welded together by the adhesive qualities of order.

System is, indeed, one of the great fundamental principles in progress, and in the binding together, in one complete whole, of the world's millions of human beings while they are at the same time each striving for a place, and are competing with one another in opposing aims and interests.

We see here how system is allied with greatness, for the many separate units whose minds are untrained to the discipline of system, are kept in their places by the organizing power of the comparatively few who perceive the urgent, the unescapable, necessity for the establishment of fixed and inviolable rules, whether in business, law, religion, science, or politics—in fact, in every sphere of human activity; for immediately two human beings meet together, they need some common ground of understanding for the avoidance of confusion; in a word, some *system* to regulate their actions.

Life is too short for confusion; and knowledge grows and progress proceeds along avenues of system which prevent retardation and retrogression, so that he who systematizes his knowledge or business, simplifies and enhances it for his successor, enabling him to begin, with a free mind, where he left off.

Every large business has its system which renders its vast machinery workable, enabling it to run like a well-balanced and well-oiled machine. A remarkable business man, a friend of mine, once told me that he could leave his huge business for twelve months, and it would run on without a hitch till his return; and he does occasionally leave it for several months, while travelling, and on his return, every man, boy, and girl; every tool, book, and machine; every detail down to the smallest, is in its place doing its work as when he left; and no trouble, no difficulty, no confusion has arisen.

There can be no marked success apart from a love of regularity and discipline, and the avoidance of friction, along with the restfulness and efficiency of mind which spring from such regularity. People who abhor discipline, whose minds are ungoverned and anarchic, and who are careless and irregular in their thinking, their habits, and the management of their affairs, cannot be highly successful and prosperous, and they fill their lives with numerous worries, troubles, difficulties, and petty annoyances, all of which would disappear under a proper regulation of their lives.

An unsystematic mind is an untrained mind, and it can no more cope with well-disciplined minds in the race of life than an untrained athlete can successfully compete with a carefully trained competitor in athletic races. The ill-disciplined mind, that thinks anything will do, rapidly falls behind the well-disciplined minds—who are convinced that only the best will do—in the strenuous race for the prizes of life, whether they be material, mental, or moral prizes. The man who, when he comes to do his work, is unable to find his tools, or to balance his figures, or to find the key of his desk, or the key to his thoughts, will be struggling in his self-made toils while his methodical neighbour will be freely and joyfully scaling the invigorating heights of successful achievement. The business man whose method is slovenly, or cumbersome, or behind the most recent developments of skilled minds, should only blame himself if his prospects are decadent, and should wake up to the necessity for more highly specialized and effective methods in his concern. He should seize upon everything— every invention and idea—that will enable him to economize time and labour, and aid him in thoroughness, deliberation, and dispatch.

System is the law by which everything—every organism, business, character, nation, empire—is built. By adding cell to cell, department to department, thought to thought, law to law, and colony to colony in orderly sequence and classification, all things, concerns, and institutions grow in magnitude and evolve to completeness. The man who is continually improving his methods, is gaining in building power; it therefore behooves the business man to be resourceful and inventive in the improvement of his methods, for the builders— whether of cathedrals or characters, businesses or religions—are the strong ones of the earth, and the protectors and pioneers of humanity. The systematic builder is a creator and preserver, while the man of disorder demolishes and destroys; and no limit can be set to the growth of a man's powers, the completeness of his character, the influence of his organization, or the extent of his business, if he but preserve intact the discipline of order, and have every detail in its place, keep every department to its special task, and tabulate and classify with such efficiency and perfection as to enable him at any moment to bring under examination or into requisition the remotest detail in connection with his special work.

In System are contained these four ingredients:

1. Readiness.
2. Accuracy.
3. Utility.
4. Comprehensiveness.

✦ Readiness ✦

Readiness is *aliveness*. It is that spirit of alertness by which a situation is immediately grasped and dealt with. The observance of system fosters and develops this spirit. The successful general must have the power of readily meeting any new and unlooked-for move on the part of the enemy; so every business man must have the readiness to deal with any unexpected development affecting his line of trade; and so also must the man of thought be able to deal with the details of any new problem which may arise. Dilatoriness is a vice that is fatal to prosperity, for it leads to incapability and stupidity. The men of ready hands, ready hearts, and ready brains, who know what they are doing, and do it methodically, skilfully, and with smooth yet consummate despatch, are the men who need to think little of prosperity, as an end, for it comes to them whether they seek it or not; success runs after them, and knocks at their door; and they unconsciously command it by the superb excellence of their faculties and methods.

✦ Accuracy ✦

Accuracy is of supreme importance in all commercial concerns and enterprises, but there can be no accuracy apart from system, and a system which is more or less imperfect will involve its originator in mistakes more or less disastrous until he improves it.

Inaccuracy is one of the commonest failings, because accuracy is closely allied to self-discipline, and self-discipline, along with that glad subjection to external discipline which it involves, is an indication of high moral culture to which the majority have not yet attained. If the inaccurate man will not willingly subject himself to the discipline of his employer or instructor, but thinks he knows better, his failing can never be remedied, and he will thereby bind himself down to an inferior position if in the business world; or to imperfect knowledge if in the world of thought.

The prevalence of the vice of inaccuracy (and in view of its disastrous effects it must be regarded as a vice, though perhaps one of the lesser vices) is patent to every observer in the way in which the majority of people relate a circumstance or repeat a simple statement of fact. It is nearly always made untrue by more or less marked inaccuracies. Few people, perhaps (not reckoning those who deliberately lie), have trained themselves to be accurate in what they say, or are so careful as to admit and state their liability to error, and from this common form of inaccuracy many untruths and misunderstandings arise.

More people take more pains to be accurate in what they do than in what they say, but even here inaccuracy is very common, rendering many inefficient and incompetent, and unfitting them for any strenuous and well-sustained endeavour. The man who habitually uses up a portion of his own or his employer's time in trying to correct his errors, or for the correction of whose mistakes another has to be employed, is not the man to maintain any position in the work-a-day world; much less to reach a place among the ranks of the prosperous.

There never yet lived a man who did not make some mistakes on his way to his particular success, but he is the capable and right-minded man who perceives his mistakes and quickly remedies them, and who is glad when they are pointed out to him. It is habitual and persistent inaccuracy which is a vice; and he is the incapable and wrong-minded man who will not see or admit his mistakes, and who takes offence when they are pointed out to him.

The progressive man learns by his own mistakes as well as by the mistakes of others. He is always ready to test good advice by practice, and aims at greater and ever greater accuracy in his methods, which means higher and higher perfection; for accuracy is perfection, and the measure of a man's accuracy will be the measure of his uniqueness and perfection.

✦ Utility ✦

Utility, or usefulness, is the direct result of method in one's work. Labour arrives at fruitful and profitable ends when it is systematically pursued. If the gardener is to gather in the best produce, he must not only sow and plant, but he must sow and plant at the right time; and if any work is to be fruitful in results, it must be done seasonably, and the time for doing a thing must not be allowed to pass by.

Utility considers the practical end, and employs the best means to reach that end. It avoids side issues, dispenses with theories, and retains its hold only on those things which can be appropriated to good uses in the economy of life.

Unpractical people burden their minds with useless and unverifiable theories, and court failure by entertaining speculations which, by their very nature, cannot be applied in practice. The man whose powers are shown in what he does, and not in mere talking and arguing, avoids metaphysical quibblings and quandaries, and applies himself to the accomplishment of some good and useful end.

That which cannot be reduced to practice should not be allowed to hamper the mind. It should be thrown aside, abandoned, and ignored. A man recently told me that if his theory should be proved to have no useful end, he should still retain his hold upon it as a beautiful theory. If a man chooses to cling to so-called "beautiful" theories which are proved to have no use in life, and no substantial basis of reality, he must not be surprised if he fail in his worldly undertakings, for he is an unpractical man.

When the powers of the mind are diverted from speculative theorizing to practical doing, whether in material or moral directions, skill, power, knowledge, and prosperity increase. A man's prosperity is measured by his usefulness to the community, and a man is useful in accordance with what he does, and not because of the theories which he entertains.

The carpenter fashions a chair; the builder erects a house; the mechanic produces a machine; and the wise man moulds a perfect character. Not the schismatics, the theorists, and the controversialists, but the workers, the makers, and the doers, are the salt of the earth.

Let a man turn away from the mirages of intellectual speculation, and begin to *do* something, and to do it with all his might, and he will thereby gain a special knowledge, wield a special power, and reach his own unique position and prosperity among his fellows.

✦ Comprehensiveness ✦

Comprehensiveness is that quality of mind which enables a man to deal with a large number of related details, to grasp them in their entirety, along with the single principle which governs them and binds them together. It is a masterly quality, giving organizing and governing power, and is developed by systematic attention to details. The successful merchant holds in his mind, as it were, all the details of his business, and regulates them by a system adapted to his particular form of trade.

The inventor has in his mind all the details of his machine, along with their relation to a central mechanical principle, and so perfects his invention. The author of a great poem or story relates all his characters and incidents to a central plot, and so produces a composite and enduring literary work. Comprehensiveness is analytic and synthetic capacity combined in the same individual. A capacious and well-ordered mind, which holds within its silent depths an army of details in their proper arrangement and true working order, is the mind that is near to genius, even if it has not already arrived. Every man cannot be a genius, nor does he need to be, but he can be gradually evolving his mental capacity by careful attention to system in his thoughts and business, and as his intellect deepens and broadens, his powers will be intensified and his prosperity accentuated.

Such, then, are the four corner Pillars in the Temple of Prosperity, and of themselves they are sufficient permanently to sustain it without the addition of the remaining four. The man who perfects himself in Energy, Economy, Integrity, and System will achieve an enduring success in the work of his life, no matter what the nature of that work may be. It is impossible for one to fail who is full of energy, who carefully economizes his time and money and virtuously husbands his vitality, who practises unswerving integrity, and who systematizes his work by first systematizing his mind.

Such a man's efforts will be rightly directed, and that, too, with concentrated power, so that they will be effective and fruitful. In addition he will reach a manliness and an independent dignity which will unconsciously command respect and success, and will strengthen weaker ones by its very presence in their midst. "Seest thou a man diligent in business; he shall stand before kings, he shall not stand before mean men," says a scripture of such a one. He will not beg, or whimper, or complain, or cynically blame others, but will be too strong and pure and upright a man to sink himself so low. And so, standing high in the nobility and integrity of his character, he will fill a high place in the world and in the estimation of men. His success will be certain and his prosperity will endure. "He will stand and not fall in the battle of life."

FIFTH PILLAR
Sympathy

The remaining pillars are the four central pillars in the temple of prosperity. They give it greater strength and stability, and add both to its beauty and utility. They contribute greatly to its attractiveness, for they belong to the highest moral sphere, and therefore to great beauty and nobility of character. They, indeed, make a man great, and place him among the comparatively few whose minds are rare, and that shine apart in sparkling purity and bright intelligence.

Sympathy should not be confounded with that maudlin and superficial sentiment which, like a pretty flower without root, presently perishes and leaves behind neither seed nor fruit. To fall into hysterical weeping when parting with a friend, or on hearing of some suffering abroad, is not sympathy. Neither are bursts of violent indignation against the cruelties and injustices of others any indication of a sympathetic mind. If one is cruel at home—if he badgers his wife, or beats his children, or abuses his servants, or stabs his neighbours with shafts of bitter sarcasm—what hypocrisy is in his profession of love for suffering people who are outside the immediate range of his influence! What shallow sentiment informs his bursts of indignation against the injustices and hard-heartedness in the world around him!

Says Emerson of such: "Go love thy infant; love thy wood-chopper: be good-natured and modest: have that grace; and never varnish your hard, uncharitable ambition with this incredible tenderness for black folk a thousand miles off. Thy love afar is spite at home." The test of a man is in his immediate acts, and not in his ultra sentiments; and if those acts are consistently informed with selfishness and bitterness,—if those at home hear his steps with dread, and feel a joyful relief on his departure—how empty are his expressions of sympathy for the suffering or down-trodden! How futile his membership of a philanthropic society!

Though the well of sympathy may feed the spring of tears, that spring more often draws its supply from the dark pool of selfishness, for when selfishness is thwarted it spends itself in tears.

Sympathy is a deep, silent, inexpressible tenderness which is shown in a consistently self-forgetful, gentle character. Sympathetic people are not gushing and spasmodic, but are permanently self-restrained, firm, quiet, unassuming and gracious. Their undisturbed demeanour where the suffering of others is concerned is frequently mistaken for indifference by shallow minds, but the sympathetic and discerning eye recognizes, in their quiet strength and their swiftness to aid while others are weeping and wringing their hands, the deepest, soundest sympathy.

Lack of sympathy is shown in cynicism, ill-natured sarcasm, bitter ridicule, taunting and mockery, and anger and condemnation, as well as in that morbid and false sentiment which is a theoretical and assumed sympathy, having no basis in practice.

Lack of sympathy arises in egotism; sympathy arises in love. Egotism is involved in ignorance; love is allied to knowledge. It is common with men to imagine themselves as separate from their fellows, with separate aims and interests; and to regard themselves as right and others wrong in their respective ways. Sympathy lifts a man above this separate and self-centred life, and enables him to live in the hearts of his fellows, and to think and feel with them. He puts himself in their place, and becomes, for the time being, as they are. As Whitman, the hospital hero, expresses it: "I do not ask the wounded person how he feels; I myself become the wounded person." It is a kind of impertinence to question a suffering creature. Suffering calls for aid and tenderness, and not for curiosity; and the sympathetic man or woman feels the suffering, and ministers to its alleviation.

Nor can sympathy boast, and wherever self-praise enters in, sympathy passes out. If one speaks of his many deeds of kindness, and complains of the ill-treatment he has received in return, he has not done kindly deeds, but has yet to reach that self-forgetful modesty which is the sweetness of sympathy.

Sympathy, in its real and profound sense, is oneness with others in their strivings and sufferings, so that the man of sympathy is a composite being; he is, as it were, a number of men, and he views a thing from a number of different sides, and not from one side only, and that his own particular side. He sees with other men's eyes, hears with their ears, thinks with their minds, and feels with their hearts. He is thus able to understand men who are vastly different from himself; the meaning of their lives is revealed to him, and he is united to them in the spirit of goodwill. Said Balzac: "The poor fascinate me; their hunger is my hunger; I am with them in their homes; their privations I suffer; I feel the beggar's rags upon my back; I for the time being become the poor and despised man." It reminds us of the saying of one greater than Balzac, that a deed done for a suffering little one was done for him.

And so it is; sympathy leads us to the hearts of all men, so that we become spiritually united to them, and when they suffer we feel the pain; when they are glad we rejoice with them; when they are despised and persecuted, we spiritually descend with them into the depths, and take into our hearts their humiliation and distress; and he who has this binding, uniting spirit of sympathy, can never be cynical and condemnatory, can never pass thoughtless and cruel judgments upon his fellows, because in his tenderness of heart he is ever with them in their pain.

But to have reached this ripened sympathy, it must needs be that one has loved much, suffered much, and sounded the dark depths of sorrow. It springs from acquaintance with the profoundest experiences, so that a man has had conceit, thoughtlessness, and selfishness burnt out of his heart. No man can have true sympathy who has not been, in some measure at least, "a man of sor-

rows, and acquainted with grief," but the sorrow
and grief must have passed, must have ripened
into a fixed kindness and habitual calm.

To have suffered so much in a certain direction that the suffering is finished, and only its particular wisdom remains, enables one, wherever
that suffering presents itself, to understand and
deal with it by pure sympathy; and when one has
been "perfected by suffering" in many directions,
he becomes a centre of rest and healing for the
sorrowing and broken-hearted who are afflicted
with the afflictions which he has experienced and
conquered. As a mother feels the anguish of her
suffering child, so the man of sympathy feels the
anguish of suffering men.

Such is the highest and holiest sympathy, but
a sympathy much less perfect is a great power for
good in human life, and a measure of it is everywhere and every day needed. While rejoicing in
the fact that in every walk in life there are truly
sympathetic people, one also perceives that harshness, resentment, and cruelty are all too common.
These hard qualities bring their own sufferings,
and there are those who fail in their business, or
particular work, entirely because of the harshness of their disposition. A man who is fiery and
resentful, or who is hard, cold, and calculating,
with the springs of sympathy dried up within him,

even though he be otherwise an able man, will, in the end, scarcely avoid disaster in his affairs. His heated folly in the one case, or cold cruelty in the other, will gradually isolate him from his fellows and from those who are immediately related to him in his particular avocation, so that the elements of prosperity will be eliminated from his life, leaving him with a lonely failure, and perhaps a hopeless despair.

Even in ordinary business transactions, sympathy is an important factor, for people will always be attracted to those who are of a kindly and genial nature, preferring to deal with them rather than with those who are hard and forbidding. In all spheres where direct personal contact plays an important part, the sympathetic man with average ability will always take precedence of the man of greater ability but who is unsympathetic.

If a man be a minister or a clergyman, a cruel laugh or an unkind sentence from him will seriously injure his reputation and influence, but particularly his influence, for even they who admire his good qualities will, through his unkindness, unconsciously have a lower regard for him in their personal esteem.

If a business man profess religion, people will expect to see the good influence of that religion on his business transactions. To profess to be a worshipper of the gentle Jesus on Sunday, and all the rest of the week be a hard, grasping worshipper of Mammon, will injure his trade, and detract considerably from his prosperity.

Sympathy is a universal spiritual language which all, even the animals, instinctively understand and appreciate, for all beings and creatures are subject to suffering, and this sameness of painful experience leads to that unity of feeling which we call sympathy.

Selfishness impels men to protect themselves at the expense of others: but sympathy impels them to protect others by the sacrifice of self; and in this sacrifice of self there is no real and ultimate loss, for while the pleasures of selfishness are small and few, the blessings of sympathy are great and manifold.

It may be asked, "How can a business man, whose object is to develop his own trade, practice self-sacrifice?" *Every man can practice self-sacrifice just where he is, and in the measure that he is capable of understanding it.* If one contends that he cannot practise a virtue because of his circumstances, he will never practise it, for were his circumstances different, he would still have the same excuse. Diligence in business is not incompatible with self-sacrifice, for devotion to duty, even though that duty be trade, is not selfishness, but may be an unselfish devotion. I know a business man who, when a competitor who had tried to "cut him out" in business, cut himself out and failed set that same competitor up in business again. Truly a beautiful act of self-sacrifice; and the man that did it is, today, one of the most successful and prosperous of business men.

The most prosperous commercial traveller I have ever known, was overflowing with exuberant kindness and geniality. He was as innocent of all "tricks of trade" as a new-born infant, but his great heart and manly uprightness won for him fast friends wherever he went. Men were glad to see him come into their office or shop or mill, and not alone for the good and bracing influence he brought with him, but also because his business was sound and trust-worthy. This man was successful through sheer sympathy, but sympathy so pure and free from policy, that he himself would probably have denied that his success could be attributed to it. Sympathy can never hinder success. It is selfishness that blights and destroys. As goodwill increases, man's prosperity will increase. All interests are mutual, and stand or fall together, and as sympathy expands the heart, it extends the circle of influence, making blessings, both spiritual and material, more greatly to abound.

Fourfold are the qualities which make up the great virtue of sympathy, namely:

1. Kindness.
2. Generosity.
3. Gentleness.
4. Insight.

✦ Kindness ✦

Kindness, when fully developed, is not a passing impulse but a permanent quality. An intermittent and unreliable impulse is not kindness, though it often goes under that name. There is no kindness in praise if it be followed by abuse. The love which seems to prompt the spontaneous kiss will be of little account if it be associated with a spontaneous spite. The gift which seemed so gracious will lose its value should the giver afterwards wish its value in return. To have one's feelings aroused to do a kind action toward another by some external stimulus pleasing to oneself, and shortly afterwards to be swayed to the other extreme toward the same person by an external event unpleasing to oneself, should be regarded as weakness of character; and it is also a selfish condition, for to do a kind action only toward one who pleases us, and when he pleases us, is to be thinking of oneself only. A true kindness is unchangeable, and needs no external stimulus to force it into action. It is a well from which thirsty souls can always drink, and it never runs dry. Kindness, when it is a strong virtue, is bestowed not only on those who please us, but also upon those whose actions go contrary to our wish and will, and it is a constant and never-varying glow of genial warmth.

There are some actions of which men repent; such are all unkind actions. There are other actions of which men do not repent, and such are all kind actions. The day comes when men are sorry for the cruel things they said and did; but the day of gladness is always with them for the kindly things they have said and done.

Unkindness mars a man's character, it mars his face as time goes on, and it mars that perfection of success which he would otherwise reach.

Kindness beautifies the character, it beautifies the face with the growth of the years, and it enables a man to reach that perfection of success to which his intellectual abilities entitle him. A man's prosperity is mellowed and enriched by the kindliness of his disposition.

✦ Generosity ✦

Generosity goes with a large-hearted kindness. If kindness be the gentle sister, Generosity is the strong brother. A free, open-handed, and magnanimous character is always attractive and influential. Stinginess and meanness always repel; they are dark, cramped, narrow, and cold. Kindness and generosity always attract; they are sunny, genial, open, and warm. That which repels makes for isolation and failure; that which attracts makes for union and success.

Giving is as important a duty as getting; and he who gets all he can, and refuses to give, will at last be unable to get; for it is as much a spiritual law that we cannot get unless we give, as that we cannot give unless we get.

Giving has always been taught as a great and important duty by all the religious teachers. This is because giving is one of the highways of personal growth and progress. It is a means by which we attain to greater and greater unselfishness, and by which we prevent the falling back into selfishness. It implies that we recognize our spiritual and social kinship with our fellowmen, and are willing to part with a portion of that we have earned or possess, for the good and well-being of others. The greedy man who, the more he gets, hungers for more still, and refuses to loosen his grasp upon his accumulating store, like a wild beast with its prey, is retrogressing; he is shutting himself out from all the higher and joy-giving qualities, and from free and life-giving communion with unselfish, happy human hearts. Dickens's Scrooge in "A Christmas Carol" represents the condition of such a man with graphic vividness and dramatic force.

Our public men in England today (probably also in America) are nearly all (I think I might say all, for I have not yet met an exception) great givers. These men—Lord Mayors, Mayors, Magistrates, Town and City Councillors, and all men filling responsible public offices—being men who have been singularly successful in the management of their own private affairs, are considered the best men for the management of public affairs, and numerous noble institutions throughout the land are perpetual witnesses to the munificence of their gifts. Nor have I been able to find any substantial truth in the accusation, so often hurled against such men by the envious and unsuccessful, that their riches are made unjustly. Without being perfect men, they are an honourable class of manly, vigorous, generous, and successful men who have acquired riches and honour by sheer industry, ability, and uprightness.

Let a man beware of greed, of meanness, of envy, of jealousy, of suspicion, for these things, if harboured, will rob him of all that is best in life, aye, even all that is best in material things, as well as all that is best in character and happiness. Let him be liberal of heart and generous of hand, magnanimous and trusting, not only giving cheerfully and often of his substance, but allowing his friends and fellow-men freedom of thought and action— let him be thus, and honour, plenty, and prosperity will come knocking at his door for admittance as his friends and guests.

✦ Gentleness ✦

Gentleness is akin to divinity. Perhaps no quality is so far removed from all that is coarse, brutal, and selfish as gentleness, so that when one is becoming gentle, he is becoming divine. It can only be acquired after much experience and through great self-discipline. It only becomes established in a man's heart when he has controlled and brought into subjection his animal passions. Its external signs are a low-pitched, clear voice, a distinct, firm, but quiet enunciation, and freedom from excitement, vehemence, or resentment in peculiarly aggravating circumstances.

If there is one quality which, above all others, should distinguish the religious man, it is the quality of gentleness, for it is the hall-mark of spiritual culture. The rudely aggressive man is an affront to cultivated minds and unselfish hearts. Our word *gentleman* has not altogether departed from its original meaning. It is still applied to one who is modest and self-restrained, and is considerate for the feelings and welfare of others. A gentle man—one whose good behaviour is prompted by thoughtfulness and kindliness—is always loved, whatever may be his origin. Quarrelsome people make a display—in their bickerings and recriminations—of their ignorance and lack of culture. The man who has perfected himself in gentleness never quarrels. He never returns the hard word; he leaves it alone, or meets it with a gentle word which is far more powerful than wrath. Gentleness is wedded to wisdom, and the wise man has overcome all anger in himself, and so understands how to overcome it in others. The gentle man is saved from most of the disturbances and turmoils with which uncontrolled men afflict themselves. While they are wearing themselves out with wasteful and needless strain, he is quiet and composed, and such quietness and composure are strong to win in the battle of life.

✦ Insight ✦

Insight is the gift of sympathy. The sympathetic mind is the profoundly perceiving mind. We understand by experience, and not by argument. Before we can know a thing or being, our life must touch its or his life. Argument analyzes the outer skin, but sympathy reaches to the heart. The cynic sees the hat and coat, and thinks he sees the man. The sympathetic seer sees the man, and is not concerned with the hat and coat. In all kinds of hatred there is a separation by which each misjudges the other. In all kinds of love there is a mystic union by which each knows the other. Sympathy, being the purest form of love, sees to the heart of men and things. Shakespeare is the greatest poet because he has the largest heart. No other figure in all literature has shown such a profound knowledge of the human heart, and of nature, both animate and inanimate. The personal Shakespeare is not to be found in his works; he is merged, by sympathy, into his characters. The wise man and the philosopher; the madman and the fool; the drunkard and the harlot—these he, for the time being, became; he stood where they stood; he entered into their particular experiences, and knew them better than they knew themselves. Shakespeare has no partiality, no prejudice; his sympathy embraces all, from the lowest to the highest.

Prejudice is the great barrier to sympathy and knowledge. It is impossible to understand those against whom one harbours a prejudice. We only see men and things as they are when we divest our minds of partial judgments. We become seers as we become sympathisers. Sympathy has knowledge for her companion.

Inseparable are the feeling heart and the seeing eye. The man of pity is the man of prophecy. He whose heart beats in tune with all hearts, to him the contents of all hearts are revealed. Nor are past and future any longer insoluble mysteries to the man of sympathy. His moral insight apprehends the perfect round of human life.

Sympathetic insight lifts a man into the consciousness of freedom, gladness, and power. His spirit inhales joy as his lungs inhale air. There are no longer any fears of his fellow-men—of competition, hard times, enemies, and the like. These groveling illusions have disappeared, and there has opened up before his awakened vision a realm of greatness and grandeur.

SIXTH PILLAR
Sincerity

Human society is held together by its sincerity. A universal falseness would beget a universal mistrust which would bring about a universal separation, if not destruction. Life is made sane, wholesome, and happy by our deep-rooted belief in one another. If we did not trust men, we could not transact business with them, could not even associate with them. Shakespeare's Timon shows us the wretched condition of a man who, through his own folly, has lost all faith in the sincerity of human nature. He cuts himself off from the company of all men, and finally commits suicide. Emerson has something to the effect that if the trust system were withdrawn from commerce, society would fall to pieces; that system being an indication of the universal confidence men place in each other. Business, commonly supposed by the short-sighted and foolish to be all fraud and deception, is based on a great trust—a trust that men will meet and fulfil their obligations. Payment is not asked until the goods are delivered; and the fact of the continuance of this system for ages, proves that most men do pay their debts, and have no wish to avoid such payment.

Back of all its shortcomings, human society rests on a strong basis of truth. Its fundamental note is sincerity. Its great leaders are all men of superlative sincerity; and their names and achievements are not allowed to perish—a proof that the virtue of sincerity is admired by all the race.

It is easy for the insincere to imagine that everybody is like themselves, and to speak of the "rottenness of society"—as though a rotten thing could endure age after age—for is not everything yellow to the jaundiced eye? People who cannot see anything good in the constitution of human society, should overhaul themselves. Their trouble is near home. They call good, evil. They have dwelt cynically and peevishly on evil till they cannot see good, and everything and everybody appear evil. "Society is rotten from top to bottom," I heard a man say recently; and he asked me if I did not think so. I replied that I should be sorry to think so; that while society had many blemishes, it was sound at the core, and contained within itself the seeds of perfection.

Society, indeed, is so sound that the man who is playing a part for the accomplishment of entirely selfish ends cannot long prosper, and cannot fill any place as an influence. He is soon unmasked and disgraced; and the fact that such a man can, for even a brief period, batten on human credulity, speaks well for the trustfulness of men, if it reveals their lack of wisdom.

An accomplished actor on the stage is admired, but the designing actor on the stage of life brings himself down to ignominy and contempt. In striving to appear what he is not, he becomes as one having no individuality, no character, and he is deprived of all influence, all power, all success.

A man of profound sincerity is a great moral force, and there is no force—not even the highest intellectual force—that can compare with it. Men are powerful in influence according to the soundness and perfection of their sincerity. Morality and sincerity are so closely bound up together, that where sincerity is lacking, morality, as a power, is lacking also, for insincerity undermines all the other virtues, so that they crumble away and become of no account. Even a little insincerity robs a character of all its nobility, and makes it common and contemptible. Falseness is so despicable a vice that it cannot co-exist with character and influence, and no man of moral weight can afford to dally with pretty compliments, or play the fool with trivial and conventional deceptions. Let a man resort to deception, howsoever light, in order to please, and he is no longer strong and admirable, but is become a shallow weakling whose mind has no deep well of power from which men can draw, and no satisfying richness to stir in them a worshipful regard.

Even they who are for the moment flattered with the painted lie, or pleased with the deftly woven deception, will not escape those permanent undercurrents of influence which move the heart and shape the judgment to fixed and final issues, while these designed delusions create but momentary ripples on the surface of the mind.

"I am very pleased with his attentions," said a woman of an acquaintance, "but I would not marry him." "Why not?" she was asked. "He doesn't ring true," was the reply.

Ring true! a term full of meaning. It has reference to the coin which, when tested by its ring, emits a sound which reveals the sterling metal throughout, without the admixture of any base material. *It comes up to the standard*, and will pass anywhere and everywhere for its full value.

So with men. Their words and actions emit their own peculiar influence. There is in them an inaudible sound which all other men inwardly hear and instinctively detect. They know the false ring from the true, yet know not how they know. As the outer ear can make the most delicate distinctions in sounds, so the inner ear can make equally subtle distinctions between souls. None are ultimately deceived but the deceiver. It is the blind folly of the insincere that, while flattering themselves upon their successful simulations, they are deceiving none but themselves. Their actions are laid bare before all hearts. There is at the heart of man a tribunal whose judgments do not miscarry. If the senses faultlessly detect, shall not the soul infallibly know! This inner infallibility is shown in the collective judgment of the race. This judgment is perfect; so perfect that in literature, art, science, invention, religion—in every department of knowledge—it divides the good from the bad, the worthy from the unworthy, the true from the false, zealously guarding and preserving the former, and allowing the latter to perish. The works, words, and deeds of great men are the heirlooms of the race, and the race is not careless of their value. A thousand men write a book, and one only is a work of original genius, yet the race singles out that one, elevates and preserves it, while it consigns the nine hundred and ninety-nine copyists to oblivion. Ten thousand men utter a sentence under a similar circumstance, and one only is a sentence of divine wisdom, yet the race singles out that saying for the guidance of posterity, while the other sentences are heard no more. It is true that the race slays its prophets, but even that slaying becomes a test which reveals the true ring, and men detect its trueness. The slain one has come up to the standard, and the deed of his slaying is preserved as furnishing infallible proof of his greatness.

As the counterfeit coin is detected, and cast back into the melting pot, while the sterling coin circulates among all men, and is valued for its worth, so the counterfeit word, deed, or character is perceived, and is left to fall back into the nothingness from which it emerged, a thing unreal, powerless, dead.

Spurious things have no value, whether they be bric-a-brac or men. We are ashamed of imitations that try to pass for the genuine article. Falseness is cheap. The masquerader becomes a byword: he is less than a man; he is a shadow, a spook, a mere mask. Trueness is valuable. The sound-hearted man becomes an exemplar: he is more than a man; he is a reality, a force, a moulding principle. By falseness all is lost—even individuality dissolves—for falseness is nonentity, nothingness. By trueness, everything is gained, for trueness is fixed, permanent, real.

It is all-important that we be real; that we harbour no wish to appear other than what we are; that we simulate no virtue, assume no excellency, adopt no disguise. The hypocrite thinks he can hoodwink the world and the eternal law of the world. There is but one person that he hoodwinks, and that is himself, and for that the law of the world inflicts its righteous penalty. There is an old theory that the excessively wicked are annihilated. I think to be a pretender is to come as near to annihilation as a man can get, for there is a sense in which the man is gone, and in his place there is but a mirage of shams. The hell of annihilation which so many dread, he has descended into; and to think that such a man can prosper is to think that shadows can do the work of entities, and displace real men.

If any man thinks he can build up a successful career on pretences and appearances, let him pause before sinking into the abyss of shadows; for in insincerity there is no solid ground, no substance, no reality; there is nothing on which anything can stand, and no material with which to build; but there are loneliness, poverty, shame, confusion, fears, suspicions, weepings, groanings, and lamentations; for if there is one hell lower, darker, fouler than all others, it is the hell of insincerity.

Four beautiful traits adorn the mind of the sincere man. They are:

1. Simplicity.
2. Attractiveness.
3. Penetration.
4. Power.

✦ Simplicity ✦

Simplicity is naturalness. It is simple being, without fake or foreign adornment. Why are all things in nature so beautiful? Because they are natural. We see them as they are, not as they might wish to appear, for in sooth they have no wish to appear otherwise. There is no hypocrisy in the world of nature outside of human nature. The flower which is so beautiful in all eyes would lose its beauty if it could pretend. Looking upon nature we look upon reality, and its beauty and perfection gladden and amaze us. We cannot find anywhere a flaw, and are conscious of our incapacity to improve upon anything, even to the most insignificant. Everything has its own peculiar perfection, and shines in the beauty of unconscious simplicity.

One of the modern social cries is "Back to nature." It is generally understood to mean a cottage in the country, and a piece of land to cultivate. It will be of little use to go into the country if we take our shams with us; and any veneer which may cling to us can as well be washed off just where we are. It is good that they who feel burdened with the conventions of society should fly to the country, and court the quiet of nature, but it will fail if it be anything but a means to that inward redemption which will restore us to the simple and the true.

But though humanity has wandered from the natural simplicity of the animal world, it is moving toward a higher, a divine simplicity. Men of great genius are such because of their spontaneous simplicity. They do not feign; they *are.* Lesser minds study style and effect. They wish to cut a striking figure on the stage of the world, and by that unholy wish they are doomed to mediocrity. Said a man to me recently, "I would give twenty years of my life to be able to write an immortal hymn." With such an ambition a man cannot write a hymn. He wants to pose. He is thinking of himself, of his own glory. Before a man can write an immortal hymn, or create any immortal work, he must give, not twenty years of his life to ambition, but his whole life to humanity. He must forget that he can do anything great, and must sing, paint, write, out of ten thousand bitter experiences, ten thousand failures, ten thousand conquests, ten thousand joys. He must know Gethsemane; he must work with blood and tears.

Retaining his intellect and moral powers, and returning to simplicity, a man becomes great. He forfeits nothing real. Only the shams are cast aside, revealing the standard gold of character. Where there is sincerity there will always be simplicity—a simplicity of the kind that we see in nature, the beautiful simplicity of truth.

✦ Attractiveness ✦

Attractiveness is the direct outcome of simplicity. This is seen in the attractiveness of all natural objects, to which we have referred, but in human nature it is manifested as *personal influence*. Of recent years certain pseudo-mystics have been advertising to sell the secret of "personal magnetism" for so many dollars, by which they purport to show vain people how they can make themselves attractive to others by certain "occult" means, as though attractiveness can be bought and sold, and put on and off like powder and paint. Nor are people who are anxious to be thought attractive, likely to become so, for their vanity is a barrier to it. The very desire to be thought attractive is, in itself, a deception, and it leads to the practice of numerous deceptions. It infers, too, that such people are conscious of lacking the genuine attractions and graces of character, and are on the lookout for a substitute; but there is no substitute for beauty of mind and strength of character. Attractiveness, like genius, is lost by being coveted, and possessed by those who are too solid and sincere of character to desire it. There is nothing in human nature—not talent, nor intellect, nor affection, nor beauty of feature,—that can compare in attractive power to that soundness of mind and wholeness of heart which we call sincerity. There is a perennial charm about a sincere man or woman, and they draw about themselves the best specimens of human nature. There can be no personal charm apart from sincerity. Infatuation there may be, and is, but this is a kind of disease, and is vastly different from the indissoluble bond by which sincere people are attached. Infatuation ends in painful disillusion, but as there is nothing hidden between sincere souls, and they stand upon that solid ground of reality, there is no illusion to be dispelled.

Leaders among men attract by the power of their sincerity, and the measure of their sincerity is the measure of their attractive influence. Howsoever great may be a man's intellect, he can never be a permanent leader and guide of men unless he be sincere. For a time he may sail jauntily upon the stream of popularity, and believe himself secure, but it is only that he may shortly fall the lower in popular odium. He cannot long deceive the people with his painted front. They will soon look behind, and find of what spurious stuff he is made. He is like a woman with a painted face. She thinks she is admired for her complexion, but all know it is paint, and despise her for it. She has one admirer—herself, and the hell of limitation to which all the insincere commit themselves is the hell of self-admiration.

Sincere people do not think of themselves—of their talent, their genius, their virtue, their beauty—and because they are so unconscious of themselves they attract all, and win their confidence, affection, and esteem.

✦ Penetration ✦

Penetration belongs to the sincere. All shams are unveiled in their presence. All simulators are transparent to the searching eye of the sincere man. With one clear glance he sees through all their flimsy pretences. Tricksters wither under his strong gaze, and want to get away from it. He who has rid his heart of all falseness, and entertains only that which is true, has gained the power to distinguish the false from the true in others. He is not deceived who is not self-deceived.

As men looking round on the objects of nature, infallibly distinguish them—such as a snake, a bird, a horse, a tree, a rose, and so on—so the sincere man distinguishes between the variety of characters. He perceives in a movement, a look, a word, an act, the nature of the man, and acts accordingly. He is on his guard without being suspicious. He is prepared for the pretender without being mistrustful. He acts from positive knowledge, and not from negative suspicion. Men are open to him, and he reads their contents. His penetrative judgment pierces to the centre of actions, and enables him to deal with them as they are. His direct and unequivocal conduct strengthens in others the good, and shames the bad, and he is a staff of strength to those who have not yet attained to his soundness of heart and head.

✦ Power ✦

Power goes with penetration. An understanding of the nature of actions is accompanied with the power to meet and deal with all actions in the right and best way. Knowledge is always power, but knowledge of the nature of actions is superlative power, and he who possesses it, becomes a Presence to all hearts, and modifies their actions for good. Long after his bodily presence has passed away, he is still a moulding force in the world, and is a spiritual reality working subtly in the minds of men, and shaping them toward sublimer ends. At first his power is local and limited, but the circle of righteousness which he has set moving continues to extend and extend till it embraces the whole world, and all men are influenced by it.

The sincere man stamps his character upon all that he does, and also upon all people with whom he comes in contact. He speaks a word in season and some one is impressed; the influence is communicated to another, and another, and presently some despairing soul ten thousand miles away hears it and is restored. Such a power is prosperity in itself, and its worth is not to be valued in coin. Money cannot purchase the priceless jewels of character, but labour in right-doing can, and he who makes himself sincere, who acquires a robust soundness throughout his entire being, will become a man of singular success and rare power.

Such is the strong Pillar of Sincerity. Its supporting power is so great that, once it is completely erected, the Temple of Prosperity is secure. Its walls will not crumble; its rafters will not decay; its roof will not fall in. It will stand while the man lives, and when he has passed away it will continue to afford a shelter and a home for others through many generations.

SEVENTH PILLAR
Impartiality

———◇———

To get rid of prejudice is a great achievement. Prejudice piles obstacles in a man's way—obstacles to health, success, happiness, and prosperity, so that he is continually running up against imaginary enemies who, when prejudice is removed, are seen to be friends. Life is, indeed, a sort of obstacle race to the man of prejudice, a race wherein the obstacles cannot be negotiated and the goal is not reached; whereas to the impartial man life is a day's walk in a pleasant country, with refreshment and rest at the end of the day.

To acquire impartiality, a man must remove that innate egotism which prevents him from seeing anything from any point of view other than his own. A great task, truly, but a noble one, and one that can be well begun now, even if it cannot be finished. Truth can "remove mountains," and prejudice is a range of mental mountains beyond which the partisan does not see, and of which he does not believe there is any beyond. These mountains removed, however, there opens to the view the unending vista of mental variety blended in one glorious picture of light and shade, of colour and tone, gladdening beholding eyes.

By clinging to stubborn prejudice what joys are missed, what friends are sacrificed, what happiness is destroyed, and what prospects are blighted! And yet freedom from prejudice is a rare thing. There are few men who are not prejudiced partisans upon the subjects which are of interest to them. One rarely meets a man that will dispassionately discuss his subject from both sides, considering all the facts and weighing all the evidence so as to arrive at truth on the matter. Each partisan has his own case to make out. He is not searching for truth, for he is already convinced that his own conclusion is the truth, and that all else is error; but he is defending his own case, and striving for victory. Neither does he attempt to prove that he has the truth by a calm array of facts and evidence, but defends his position with more or less heat and agitation.

Prejudice causes a man to form a conclusion, sometimes without any basis of fact or knowledge, and then to refuse to consider anything which does not support that conclusion; and in this way prejudice is a complete barrier to the attainment of knowledge. It binds a man down to darkness and ignorance, and prevents the development of his mind in the highest and noblest directions. More than this, it also shuts him out from communion with the best minds, and Confines him to the dark and solitary cell of his own egotism.

Prejudice is a shutting up of the mind against the entrance of new light, against the perception of more beauty, against the hearing of diviner music. The partisan clings to his little, fleeting, flimsy opinion, and thinks it the greatest thing in the world. He is so in love with his own conclusion (which is only a form of self-love) that he thinks all men ought to agree with him, and he regards men as more or less stupid who do not see as he sees, while he praises the good judgment of those who are one with him in his view. Such a man cannot have knowledge, cannot have truth. He is Confined to the sphere of opinion (to his own self-created illusions) which is outside the realm of reality. He moves in a kind of self-infatuation which prevents him from seeing the commonest facts of life, while his own theories—usually more or less ground-less—assume, in his mind, overpowering propor-tions. He fondly imagines that there is but one side to everything, and that side his own. There are at least two sides to everything, and he it is who finds the truth in a matter who carefully examines both sides with all freedom from excitement, and without any desire for the predominance of one side over another.

In its divisions and controversies the world at large is like two lawyers defending a case. The counsel for the prosecution presents all the facts which prove his side, while counsel for the defence presents all the facts which support his contention, and each belittles or ignores or tries to reason away the facts of the other. The judge in the case, however, is like the impartial thinker among men; having listened to all the evidence on both sides, he compares and sifts it so as to form an impartial summing up in the cause of justice.

Not that this universal partiality is a bad thing, for as in all other extremes, nature here reduces the oppositions of conflicting parties to a perfect balance; moreover, it is a factor in evolution; it stimulates men to think who have not yet developed the power to rouse up vigorous thought at will, and it is a phase through which all men have to pass. But it is only a byway—and a tangled, confused, and painful one—toward the great highway of Truth. It is the arc of which impartiality is the perfect round. The partisan sees a portion of the truth, and thinks it the whole, but the impartial thinker sees the whole truth which includes all sides. It is necessary that we first see truth in sections, as it were, until, having gathered up all the parts, we may piece them together and form the perfect circle; and the forming of such circle is the attainment of impartiality.

The impartial man examines, weighs, and considers, with freedom from prejudice and from likes and dislikes. His one wish is to discover the truth. He abolishes preconceived opinions, and lets facts and evidence speak for themselves. He has no case to make out for himself, for he knows that truth is unalterable, that his opinions can make no difference to it, and that it can be investigated and discovered. He thereby escapes a vast amount of friction and nervous wear and tear to which the feverish partisan is subject; and in addition, he looks directly upon the face of Reality, and so becomes tranquil and peaceful.

So rare is freedom from prejudice that wherever the impartial thinker may be, he is sure, sooner or later, to occupy a very high position in the estimation of the world, and in the guidance of its destiny. Not necessarily an office in worldly affairs, for that is improbable, but an exalted position in the sphere of influence. There may be such a one now, and he may be a carpenter, a weaver, a clerk; he may be in poverty or in the home of a millionaire; he may be short or tall, or of any complexion, but whatever and wherever he may be, he has, though unknown, already begun to move the world, and will one day be universally recognized as a new force and creative centre in evolution.

There was one such some nineteen hundred years ago. He was only a poor, unlettered carpenter; he was regarded as a madman by his own relatives, and he came to an ignominious end in the eyes of his countrymen; but he sowed the seeds of an influence which has altered the whole world.

There was another such in India some twenty-five centuries ago. He was accomplished, highly educated, and was the son of a capitalist and landed proprietor—a petty king. He became a penniless, homeless mendicant, and today one-third of the human race worship at his shrine, and are restrained and elevated by his influence.

"Beware when the great God lets loose a thinker on this planet," says Emerson; and a man is not a thinker who is bound by prejudice; he is merely the strenuous upholder of an opinion. Every idea must pass through the medium of his particular prejudice, and receive its colour, so that dispassionate thinking and impartial judgment are rendered impossible. Such a man sees everything only in its relation, or imagined relation, to his opinion, whereas the thinker sees things as they are. The man who has so purified his mind of prejudice and of all the imperfections of egotism as to be able to look directly upon reality, has reached the acme of power; he holds in his hands, as it were, the vastest influence, and he will wield this power whether he knows it or not; it will be inseparable from his life, and will go from him as perfume from the flower. It will be in his words, his deeds, in his bodily postures and the motions of his mind, even in his silence and the stillness of his frame. Wherever he goes, even though he should fly to the desert, he will not escape this lofty destiny, for a great thinker is the centre of the world; by him all men are held in their orbits, and all thought gravitates toward him.

The true thinker lives above and beyond the seething whirlpool of passion in which mankind is engulfed. He is not swayed by personal considerations, for he has grasped the import of impersonal principles, and being thus a non-combatant in the clashing warfare of egotistic desires, he can, from the vantage ground of an impartial, but not indifferent watcher, see both sides equally, and grasp the cause and meaning of the fray.

Not only the Great Teachers, but the greatest figures in literature, are those who are free from prejudice, who, like true mirrors, reflect things impartially. Such are Whitman, Shakespeare, Balzac, Emerson, Homer. These minds are not local, but universal. Their attitude is cosmic and not personal. They contain within themselves all things and beings, all worlds and laws. They are the gods who guide the race, and who will bring it at last out of its fever of passion into their own serene land.

The true thinker is the greatest of men, and his destiny is the most exalted. The altogether impartial mind has reached the divine, and it basks in the full daylight of Reality.

The four great elements of impartiality are:

1. Justice.
2. Patience.
3. Calmness.
4. Wisdom.

✦ Justice ✦

Justice is the giving and receiving of equal values. What is called "striking a hard bargain" is a kind of theft. It means that the purchaser gives value for only a portion of his purchase, the remainder being appropriated as clear gain. The seller also encourages it by closing the bargain.

The just man does not try to gain an advantage; he considers the true values of things, and moulds his transactions in accordance therewith. He does not let "what will pay" come before "what is right," for he knows that the right pays best in the end. He does not seek his own benefit to the disadvantage of another, for he knows that a just action benefits, equally and fully, both parties to a transaction. If "one man's loss is another man's gain," it is only that the balance may be adjusted later on. Unjust gains cannot lead to prosperity, but are sure to bring failure. A just man could no more take from another an unjust gain by what is called a "smart transaction" than he could take it by picking his pocket. He would regard the one as dishonest as the other.

The bargaining spirit in business is not the true spirit of commerce. It is the selfish and thieving spirit which wants to get something for nothing. The upright man purges his business of all bargaining, and builds it on the more dignified basis of justice. He supplies "a good article" at its right price, and does not alter. He does not soil his hands with any business which is tainted with fraud. His goods are genuine and they are properly priced.

Customers who try to "beat down" a tradesman in their purchases, are degrading themselves. Their practice assumes one or both of two things; namely, that either the tradesman is dishonest and is overcharging (a low, suspicious attitude of mind), or that they are eager to cajole him out of his profit (an equally base attitude) and so benefit by his loss. The practice of "beating down" is altogether a dishonest one, and the people who pursue it most assiduously are those who complain most of being "imposed on"; and this is not surprising, seeing that they themselves are all the time trying to impose upon others.

On the other hand, the tradesman who is anxious to get all he can out of his customers, irrespective of justice and the right values of things, is a kind of robber, and is slowly poisoning his success, for his deeds will assuredly come home to him in the form of financial ruin.

Said a man of fifty to me the other day, "I have just discovered that all my life I have been paying fifty per cent more for everything than I ought to." A just man cannot feel that he has ever paid too much for anything, for he does not close with any transaction which he considers unjust; but if a man is eager to get everything at half-price, then he will be always meanly and miserably mourning that he is paying double for everything. The just man is glad to pay full value for everything, whether in giving or receiving, and his mind is untroubled and his days are full of peace.

Let a man above all avoid meanness, and strive to be ever more and more perfectly just, for if not just, he can be neither honest, nor generous, nor manly, but is a kind of disguised thief trying to get all he can, and give back as little as possible. Let him eschew all bargaining, and teach bargainers a better way by conducting his business with that exalted dignity which commands a large and meritorious success.

✦ Patience ✦

Patience is the brightest jewel in the character of the impartial man. Not a particular patience with a particular thing—like a girl with her needlework, or a boy building his toy engine—but an unswerving considerateness, a sweetness of disposition at all times and under the most trying circumstances, an unchangeable gentle strength which no trial can mar and no persecution can break. A rare possession, it is true, and one not to be expected for a long time yet from the bulk of mankind, but a virtue that can be reached by degrees; and even a partial patience will work wonders in a man's life and affairs, as a confirmed impatience will work devastation. The irascible man is courting speedy disaster, for who will care to deal with a man who is continually going off like gunpowder when some small spark of complaint or criticism falls upon him! Even his friends will one by one desert him, for who would court the company of a man who rudely assaults him with an impatient and fiery tongue over every little difference or misunderstanding!

A man must begin wisely to control himself, and to learn the beautiful lessons of patience, if he is to be highly prosperous, if he is to be a man of use and power. He must learn to think of others, to act for their good, and not alone for himself; to be considerate, forbearing, and long-suffering. He must study how to have a heart at peace with men who differ from him on those things which he regards as most vital. He must avoid quarrelling as he would avoid drinking a deadly poison. Discords from without will be continually overtaking him, but he must fortify himself against them; he must study how to bring harmonies out of them by the exercise of patience.

Strife is common: it pains the heart and distorts the mind. Patience is rare: it enriches the heart and beautifies the mind. Every cat can spit and fume; it requires no effort, but only a looseness of behaviour. It takes a *man* to keep his moorings through all events, and to be painstaking and patient with the shortcomings of humanity. But patience wins. As soft water wears away the hardest rock, so patience overcomes all opposition. It gains the hearts of men. It conquers and controls.

✦ Calmness ✦

Calmness accompanies patience. It is a great and glorious quality. It is the peaceful haven of emancipated souls after their long wanderings on the tempest-riven ocean of passion. It marks the man who has suffered much, endured much, experienced much, and has finally conquered.

A man cannot be impartial who is not calm. Excitement, prejudice, and partiality spring from disturbed passions. When personal feeling is thwarted, it rises and seethes like a stream of water that is dammed. The calm man avoids this disturbance by directing his feeling from the personal to the impersonal channel. He thinks and feels for others as well as for himself. He sets the same value on other men's opinions as on his own. If he regards his own work as important, he sees also that the work of other men is equally important. He does not contend for the merit of his own against the demerit of that of others. He is not overthrown, like Humpty-dumpty, with a sense of self-importance. He has put aside egotism for truth, and he perceives the right relations of things. He has conquered irritability, and has come to see that there is nothing in itself that should cause irritation. As well be irritable with a pansy because it is not a rose, as with a man because he does not see as you see. Minds differ, and the calm man recognizes the differences as facts in human nature.

The calm, impartial man is not only the happiest man, he also has all his powers at his command. He is sure, deliberate, executive, and swiftly and easily accomplishes in silence what the irritable man slowly and laboriously toils through with much noise. His mind is purified, poised, concentrated, and is ready at any moment to be directed upon a given work with unerring power. In the calm mind all passions are tranquillized, all conflicts are harmonized, all contradictions are reconciled, and there is radiant gladness and perpetual peace. As Emerson puts it, "Calmness is joy fixed and habitual."

One should not confound indifference with calmness, for it is at the opposite extreme. Indifference is lifelessness, while calmness is glowing life and full-orbed power. The calm man has partly or entirely conquered self, and having successfully battled with the selfishness within, he knows how to meet and overcome it successfully in others. In any moral contest the calm man is always the victor. So long as he remains calm, defeat is impossible.

Self-control is better than riches, and calmness is a perpetual benediction.

✦ Wisdom ✦

Wisdom abides with the impartial man. Her counsels guide him; her wings shield him; she leads him along pleasant ways to happy destinations.

Wisdom is many-sided. The wise man adapts himself to others. He acts for their good, yet never violates the moral virtues or the principles of right conduct. The foolish man cannot adapt himself to others; he acts for himself only, and continually violates the moral virtues and the principles of right conduct. There is a degree of wisdom in every act of impartiality, and once a man has touched and experienced the impartial zone, he can recover it again and again, until he finally establishes himself in it.

Every thought, word, or act of wisdom tells on the world at large, for it is fraught with greatness. Wisdom is a well of knowledge and a spring of power. It is profound and comprehensive, and is so exact and all-inclusive as to embrace the smallest details. In its spacious greatness it does not overlook the small. The wise mind is like the world: it contains all things in their proper place and order, and is not burdened thereby. Like the world, also, it is free, and unconscious of any restrictions; yet it is never loose, never erring, never sinful and repentant. Wisdom is the steady, grown-up being of whom folly was the crying infant. It has outgrown the weakness and dependence, the errors and punishments of infantile ignorance, and is erect, poised, strong, and serene.

The understanding mind needs no external support. It stands of itself on the firm ground of knowledge; not book knowledge, but ripened experience. It has passed through all minds, and therefore knows them. It has traveled with all hearts, and knows their journeyings in joy and sorrow.

When wisdom touches a man, he is lifted up and transfigured. He becomes a new being, with new aims and powers, and he inhabits a new universe in which to accomplish a new and glorious destiny.

Such is the Pillar of Impartiality which adds its massive strength and incomparable grace to support and beautify the Temple of Prosperity.

EIGHTH PILLAR
Self-Reliance

Every young man ought to read Emerson's essay on " Self-reliance." It is the manliest, most virile essay that was ever penned. It is calculated to cure alike those two mental maladies common to youth; namely, self-depreciation and self-conceit. It is almost as sure to reveal to the prig the smallness and emptiness of his vanity, as it is to show the bashful man the weakness and ineffectuality of his diffidence. It is a new revelation of manly dignity: as much a revelation as any that was vouchsafed to ancient seer and prophet, and perhaps a more practical, eminently suited to this mechanic age, coming as it does from a modern prophet of a new type and cradled in a new race; and its chief merit is its powerfully tonic quality.

Let not self-reliance be confounded with self-conceit, for as high and excellent as is the one, just so low and worthless is the other. There cannot be anything mean in self-reliance, while in self-conceit there cannot be anything great.

The man that never says "no" when questioned on subjects of which he is entirely ignorant, to avoid, as he imagines, being thought ignorant, but confidently puts forward guesses and assumptions as knowledge, will be known for his ignorance and ill-esteemed for his added conceit. An honest confession of ignorance will command respect where a conceited assumption of knowledge will elicit contempt.

The timid, apologetic man who seems almost afraid to live, who fears that he will do something not in the approved way, and will subject himself to ridicule, is not a full man. He must needs imitate others, and have no independent action. He needs that self-reliance which will compel him to fall back on his own initiative, and so become a new example instead of the slavish follower of an old one. As for ridicule—he who is hurt by it is no man. The shafts of mockery and sarcasm cannot pierce the strong armour of the self-reliant man, they cannot reach the invincible citadel of his honest heart to sting or wound it. The sharp arrows of irony may rain upon him, but he laughs as they are deflected by the strong breastplate of his confidence and fall harmless about him.

"Trust thyself," says Emerson; "every heart vibrates to that iron string." Throughout the ages men have so far leaned, and do still lean, upon external makeshifts instead of standing upon their own native simplicity and original dignity. The few who have had the courage so to stand, have been singled out and elevated as heroes; and he is indeed the true hero who has the hardihood to let his nature speak for itself, who has that strong metal which enables him to stand upon his own intrinsic worth.

It is true that the candidate for such heroism must endure the test of strength. He must not be shamed from his ground by the bugbears of an imitative conventionalism. He must not fear for his reputation or position, or for his standing in the Church or his prestige in local society. He must learn to act and live as independently of these considerations as he does of the current fashions in the antipodes. Yet when he has endured this test, and slander and odium have failed to move or afflict him, he has become a man indeed, one that society will have to reckon with, and finally accept on his own terms.

Sooner or later all men turn for guidance to the self-reliant man, and while the best minds do not make a prop of him, they respect and value his work and worth, and recognize his place among the gods that have gone before.

It must not be thought an indication of self-reliance to scorn to learn. Such an attitude is born of a stubborn superciliousness which has the elements of weakness, and is prophetic of a fall, rather than the elements of strength and the promise of high achievement which are characteristic of self-reliance. Pride and vanity must not be associated with self-reliance. Those degrade, while this ennobles. Pride rests upon incidentals and appurtenances—on money, clothing, property, prestige, position—and these lost, all is lost. Self-reliance rests upon essentials and principles—on worth, probity, purity, sincerity, character, truth—and whatever may be lost is of little account, for these are never lost. Pride tries to hide its ignorance by ostentation and assumption, and is unwilling to be thought a learner in any direction. It stands, during its little fleeting day, on ignorance and appearance, and the higher it is lifted up today, the lower will it be cast down to-morrow. Self-reliance has nothing to hide, and is willing to learn; and while there can be no humility where pride is, self-reliance and humility are compatible, nay

more, they are complementary, and the sublimest form of self-reliance is only found associated
with the profoundest humility. "Extremes meet,"
says Emerson, "and there is no better example
than the haughtiness of humility. No aristocrat,
no prince born to the purple, can begin to compare with the self-respect of the saint. Why is he
so lowly, but that he knows that he can well afford
it, resting on the largeness of God in him?" It was
Buddha who, in this particular, said: "Those who,
either now or after I am dead, shall be a lamp
unto themselves, relying upon themselves only
and not relying upon any external help, but holding fast to the truth as their lamp, and seeking
their salvation in the truth alone, shall not look
for assistance to any one besides themselves, it
is they, among my disciples, who shall reach the
very topmost height! But they must be willing
to learn." In this saying, the repeated insistence
on the necessity for relying upon oneself alone,
coupled with the final exhortation to be eager to
learn, is the wisest utterance on self-reliance that
I know. In it, the Great Teacher comprehends that
perfect balance between self-trust and humility
which the man of truth must acquire.

"Self-trust is the essence of heroism." All great
men are self-reliant, and we should use them as
teachers and exemplars, and not as props and per-

ambulators. A great man comes who leans upon no one, but stands alone in the solitary dignity of truth, and straightway the world begins to lean upon him, begins to make him an excuse for spiritual indolence and a destructive self-abasement. Better than cradling our vices in the strength of the great would it be newly to light our virtues at their luminous lamp. If we rely upon the light of another, darkness will overtake us, but if we rely upon our own light we have but to keep it burning. We may both draw light from another and communicate it, but to think it sufficient while our own lamp is rusting in neglect, is shortly to find ourselves abandoned in darkness. Our own inner light is the light which never fails us.

What is the "inner light" of the Quakers but another name for self-reliance? We should stand upon what we are, not upon what another is. "But I am so small and poor," you say: well, stand upon that smallness, and presently it will become great. A babe must needs suckle and cling, but not so a man. Henceforth he goes upon his own limbs. Men pray to God to put into their hands that which they are framed to reach out for; to put into their mouths the food for which they should strenuously labour. But men will outgrow this spiritual infancy. The time will come when men will no more pay a priest to pray for them and preach to them.

Man's chief trouble is a mistrust of himself, so that the self-trusting man becomes a rare and singular spectacle. If a man look upon himself as a "worm," what can come out of him but an ineffectual wriggling! Truly, "He that humbleth himself shall be exalted" but not he that degradeth himself. A man should see himself as he is, and if there is any unworthiness in him, he should get rid of it, and retain and rely upon that which is of worth. A man is only debased when he debases himself; he is exalted when he lives an exalted life.

Why should a man, with ceaseless iterations, draw attention to his fallen nature? There is a false humility which takes a sort of pride in vice. If one has fallen, it is that he may rise and be the wiser for it. If a man falls into a ditch, he does not lie there and call upon every passer-by to mark his fallen state; he gets up and goes on his way with greater care. So if one has fallen into the ditch of vice, let him rise and be cleansed, and go on his way rejoicing.

There is not a sphere in life wherein a man's influence and prosperity will not be considerably increased by even a measure of self-reliance, and to the teacher—whether secular or religious—to organizers, managers, overseers, and all in positions of control and command, it is an indispensable quality.

The four grand qualities of self-reliance are:

1. Decision.
2. Steadfastness.
3. Dignity.
4. Independence.

✦ Decision ✦

Decision makes a man strong. The waverer is the weakling. A man who is to play a speaking part, howsoever small, in the drama of life must be decisive and know what he is about. Whatever he doubts, he must not doubt his power to act. He must know his part in life, and put all his energy into it. He must have some solid ground of knowledge from which to work, and stand securely on that. It may be only the price and quality of stock, but he must know his work thoroughly, and know that he knows it. He must be ready at any time to answer for himself when his duty is impugned. He should be so well grounded upon his particular practice as not to be afflicted with hesitation on any point or in any emergency. It is a true saying that "the man that hesitates is lost." No one believes in him who does not believe in himself, who doubts, halts, and wavers, and cannot extricate himself from the tangled threads of two courses. Who would deal with a tradesman who did not know the price of his own goods, or was not sure where to find them? A man must know his business. If he does not know his own, who shall instruct him? He must be able to give a good report of the truth that is in him, must have that decisive touch which skill and knowledge only can impart.

Certainty is a great element in self-reliance. To have weight, a man must have some truth to impart, and all skill is a communication of truth. He must "speak with authority, and not as the scribes." He must master something, and know that he has mastered it, so as to deal with it lucidly and understandingly, in the way of a master, and not to remain always an apprentice.

Indecision is a disintegrating factor. A minute's faltering may turn back the current of success. Men who are afraid to decide quickly for fear of making a mistake, nearly always make a mistake when they do act. The quickest, in thought and action, are less liable to blunder, and it is better to act with decision and make a mistake than to act with indecision and make a mistake, for in the former case there is but error, but in the latter, weakness is added to error.

A man should be decided always, both where he knows and where he does not know. He should be as ready to say no as yes, as quick to acknowledge his ignorance as to impart his knowledge.

If he stands upon fact, and acts from the simple truth, he will find no room for halting between two opinions.

Make up your mind quickly, and act decisively. Better still, have a mind that is already made up, and then decision will be instinctive and spontaneous.

✦ Steadfastness ✦

Steadfastness arises in the mind that is quick to decide. It is, indeed, a final decision upon the best course of conduct and the best path in life. It is the vow of the soul to stand firmly by its principles whatever betide. It is neither necessary nor unnecessary that there be any written or spoken vow, for unswerving loyalty to a fixed principle is the spirit of all vows.

The man without fixed principles will not accomplish much. Expediency is a quagmire and a thorny waste, in which a man is continually sticking in the shifting mud of his own moral looseness, and is pricked and scratched with the thorns of his self-created disappointments.

One must have some solid ground on which to stand among one's fellows. We cannot stand on the bog of concession. Shiftiness is a vice of weakness, and the vices of weakness do more to undermine character and influence than the vices of strength. The man that is vicious through excess of animal strength takes a shorter cut to truth—when his mind is made up—than he who is vicious through lack of virility, and whose chief vice consists in not having a mind of his own upon anything. When one understands that power is adaptable to both good and bad ends, it will not surprise him that the drunkards and harlots should reach the kingdom of heaven before the diplomatic religionists. They are at least thorough in the course which they have adopted, vile though it be, and thoroughness is strength. It only needs that strength to be turned from bad to good, and lo! the loathed sinner has become the lofty saint!

A man should have a firm, fixed, determined mind. He should decide upon those principles which are best to stand by in all issues, and which will most safely guide him through the maze of conflicting opinions, and inspire him with unflinching courage in the battle of life. Having adopted his principles, they should be more to him than gain or happiness, more even than life itself, and if he never deserts them, he will find that they will never desert him; they will defend him from all enemies, deliver him safely from all dangers, light up his pathway through all darkness and difficulties. They will be to him a light in darkness, a resting-place from sorrow, and a refuge from the conflicts of the world.

✦ Dignity ✦

Dignity clothes, as with a majestic garment, the steadfast mind. He who is as unyielding as a bar of steel when he is expected to compromise with evil, and as supple as a willow wand in adapting himself to that which is good, carries about with him a dignity that calms and uplifts others by its presence.

The unsteady mind, the mind that is not anchored to any fixed principles, that is stubborn where its own desires are threatened, and yielding where its own moral welfare is at stake, has no gravity, no balance, no calm composure.

The man of dignity cannot be down-trodden and enslaved, because he has ceased to tread upon and enslave himself. He at once disarms, with a look, a word, a wise and suggestive silence, any attempt to demean him. His mere presence is a wholesome reproof to the flippant and the unseemly, while it is a rock of strength to the lover of the good.

But the chief reason why the dignified man commands respect is, not only that he is supremely self-respecting, but that he graciously treats all others with a due esteem. Pride loves itself, and treats those beneath it with supercilious contempt, for love of self and contempt for others are always found together in equal degrees, so that the greater the self-love, the greater the arrogance. True dignity arises, not from self-love, but from self-sacrifice—that is, from unbiased adherence to a fixed central principle. The dignity of the judge arises from the fact that in the performance of his duty he sets aside all personal considerations and stands solely upon the law; his little personality, impermanent and fleeting, becomes nothing, while the law, enduring and majestic, becomes all. Should a judge, in deciding a case, forget the law and fall into personal feeling and prejudice, his dignity would be gone. So with the man of stately purity of character, he stands upon the divine law, and not upon personal feeling; for immediately a man gives way to passion he has sacrificed dignity, and takes his place as one of the multitude of the unwise and uncontrolled.

Every man will have composure and dignity in the measure that he acts from a fixed principle. It only needs that the principle be right, and therefore unassailable. So long as a man abides by such a principle and does not waver or descend into the personal element, attacking passions, prejudices, and interests, howsoever powerful, will be weak and ineffectual before the unconquerable strength

of an incorruptible principle, and will at last yield
their combined and unseemly confusion to his single and majestic right.

✦ Independence ✦

Independence is the birthright of the strong and
well-controlled man. All men love and strive for
liberty. All men aspire to some sort of freedom.

A man should labour for himself or for the community. Unless he is a cripple, a chronic invalid, or
is mentally irresponsible, he should be ashamed to
depend upon others for all he has, giving nothing
in return. If one imagines that such a condition is
freedom, let him know that it is one of the lowest
forms of slavery. The time will come when, to be
a drone in the human hive, even (as matters are
now) a respectable drone and not a poor tramp,
will be a public disgrace and will be no longer
respectable.

Independence, freedom, glorious liberty, come
through labour and not from idleness, and the
self-reliant man is too strong, too honourable, too
upright to depend upon others, like a sucking babe,
for his support. He earns, with hand or brain, the
right to live as becomes a man and a citizen; and
this he does whether born rich or poor, for riches
are no excuse for idleness; rather are they an oppor-

tunity to labour, with the rare facilities which they afford, for the good of the community.

Only he who is self-supporting is free, self-reliant, independent.

Thus is the nature of the Eight Pillars explained. On what foundation they rest, the manner of their building, their ingredients, the fourfold nature of the material of which each is composed, what positions they occupy, and how they support the Temple,—all is made clear, so that he who knew not how to build, may now build; and he who knew but imperfectly, may know more perfectly; and he who knew perfectly may rejoice in this systematization and simplification of the moral order in Prosperity. Let us now consider the Temple itself, that we may know the might of its Pillars, the strength of its walls, the endurance of its roof, and the architectural beauty and perfection of the whole.

The Temple of Prosperity

The reader who has followed the course of this book with a view to obtaining information on the details of money-making, business transactions, profit and loss in various undertakings, prices, markets, agreements, contracts, and other matters connected with the achievement of prosperity, will have noted an entire absence of any instruction on these matters of detail. The reason for this is fourfold, namely:

First—Details cannot stand alone, but are powerless to build up anything unless intelligently related to principles.

Second—Details are Infinite and are ceaselessly changing, while principles are few and are eternal and unchangeable.

Third—Principles are the coherent factors in all details, regulating and harmonizing them, so that to have right principles is to be right in all the subsidiary details.

Fourth—A teacher of truth in any direction *must* adhere rigidly to principles, and must not allow himself to be drawn away from them into the everchanging maze of private particulars and personal details, because such particulars and details have only a local right and are only necessary for certain individuals, while principles are universally right and are necessary for all men.

He who grasps the principles of this book so as to be able intelligently to practice them, will be able to reach the heart of this fourfold reason. The details of a man's affairs are important, but they are *his* details, or the details of his particular branch of industry, and all outside that branch are not concerned with them; but moral principles are the same for all men, they are applicable to all conditions and govern all particulars.

The man who works from fixed principles does not need to harass himself over the complications of numerous details. He will grasp, as it were, the entire details in one single thought, and will see them through and through, illumined by the light of the principle to which they stand related, and this without friction, and with freedom from anxiety and strain.

Until principles are grasped, details are regarded, and dealt with, as primary matters, and so viewed they lead to innumerable complications and confused issues. In the light of principles, they are seen to be secondary facts, and so seen, all difficulties connected with them are at once overcome and annulled by a reference to principles.

He who is involved in numerous details without the regulating and synthesizing element of principles is like one lost in a forest, with no direct path along which to walk amid the mass of objects. He is swallowed up by the details, while the man of principles contains all details within himself: he stands outside them, as it were, and grasps them in their entirety, while the other man can only see the few that are nearest to him at the time.

All things are contained in principles. They are the laws of things, and all things observe their own law. It is an error to view things apart from their nature. Details are the letter of which principles are the spirit. It is as true in art, science, literature, commerce, as in religion that "the letter killeth, the spirit giveth life." The body of a man, with its wonderful combinations of parts, is important, but only in its relation to the spirit. The spirit being withdrawn, the body is useless and is put away. The body of a business, with all its complicated details, is important, but only in its relation to the vivifying principles by which it is controlled. These withdrawn, the business will perish.

To have the body of prosperity—its material presentation—we must first have the spirit of prosperity, and the spirit of prosperity is the quick spirit of moral virtue. Moral blindness prevails. Men see money, property, pleasure, leisure, etc., and, mistaking them for prosperity, strive to get them for their own enjoyment; but, when obtained, they find no enjoyment in them.

Prosperity is at first a spirit, an attitude of mind, a moral power, a life, which manifests outwardly in the form of plenty, happiness, joy. Just as a man cannot become a genius by writing poems, essays, plays, but must develop and acquire the soul of genius—when the writing will follow as effect to cause—so one cannot become prosperous by hoarding up money, and by gaining property and possessions, but must develop and acquire the soul of virtue—when the material accessories will follow as effect to cause—for the spirit of virtue is the spirit of joy, and it contains within itself all abundance, all satisfaction, all fulness of life.

There is no joy in money, there is no joy in property, there is no joy in material accumulations or in any material thing of itself. These things are dead and lifeless. The spirit of joy must be in the man or it is nowhere. He must have within him the capacity for happiness. He must have the wisdom to know how to use these things, and not merely hoard them. He must possess them, and not be possessed by them. They must be dependent upon him, and not he upon them. They must follow him, and not he forever be running after them; and they will inevitably follow him, if he have the moral elements within to which they are related.

Nothing is absent from the kingdom of heaven; it contains all good, true, and necessary things, and "the kingdom of God is within you." I know rich people who are supremely happy, because they are generous, magnanimous, pure, and joyful; but I also know rich people who are very miserable, and these are they who looked to money and possessions for their happiness, and have not developed the spirit of good and of joy within themselves.

How can it be said of a wretched man that he is "prosperous," even if his income be ten thousand

pounds a year? There must be fitness, and harmony, and satisfaction in a true prosperity. When
a rich man is happy, it is that he brought the spirit
of happiness to his riches, and not that the riches
brought happiness to him. He is a full man with
full material advantages and responsibilities, while
the miserable rich man is an empty man looking
to riches for that fulness of life which can only be
evolved from within.

Thus prosperity resolves itself into a moral
capacity, and in the wisdom to use rightfully and
enjoy lawfully the material things which are inseparable from our earthly life. If one would be free
without, let him first be free within, for if he be
bound in spirit by weakness, selfishness, or vice,
how can the possession of money liberate him!
Will it not rather become, in his hands, a ready
instrument by which further to enslave himself?

The visible effects of prosperity, then, must not
be considered alone, but in their relation to the
mental and moral cause. There is a hidden foundation to every building; the fact that it continues
to stand is proof of that. There is a hidden foundation to every form of established success; its perma-
nence proves that it is so. Prosperity stands on the
foundation of *character*, and there is not, in all the
wide universe, any other foundation. True wealth
is weal, welfare, well-being, soundness, wholeness,

and happiness. The wretched rich are not truly wealthy. They are merely encumbered with money, luxury, and leisure, as instruments of self-torture. By their possessions they are self-cursed.

The moral man is ever blessed, ever happy, and his life viewed as a whole is always a success. To this there is no exception, for whatever failures he may have in detail, the finished work of his life will be sound, whole, complete; and through all he will have a quiet conscience, an honourable name, and all manifold blessings which are inseparable from richness of character, and without this moral richness, financial riches will not avail or satisfy.

Let us briefly recapitulate, and again view the Eight Pillars in their strength and splendour.

1. **Energy:** Rousing oneself up to strenuous and unremitting exertion in the accomplishment of one's task.

2. **Economy:** Concentration of power; the conservation of both capital and character, the latter being mental capital, and therefore of the utmost importance.

3. **Integrity:** Unswerving honesty; keeping inviolate all promises, agreements, and contracts, apart from all considerations of loss or gain.

4. **System:** Making all details subservient to order, and thereby relieving the memory and the mind of superfluous work and strain by reducing many to one.

5. **Sympathy:** Magnanimity, generosity, gentleness, and tenderness; being open-handed, free, and kind.

6. **Sincerity:** Being sound and whole, robust and true; and therefore not being one person in public and another in private, and not assuming good actions openly while doing bad actions in secret.

7. **Impartiality:** Justice; not striving for self, but weighing both sides, and acting in accordance with equity.

8. **Self-reliance:** Looking to oneself only for strength and support by standing on principles which are fixed and invincible, and not relying upon outward things which at any moment may be snatched away.

How can any life be other than successful which is built on these Eight Pillars? Their strength is such that no physical or intellectual strength can compare with it; and to have built all the eight perfectly would render a man invincible. It will be found, however, that men are often strong in one or several of these qualities, and weak in others; and it is this weak element that invites the ignorant to attribute, for instance, a man's failure in business to his honesty. It is impossible for honesty to produce failure. The cause of failure must be looked for in some other direction—in the lack, and not the possession, of some good and necessary quality. Moreover, such attribution of failure to honesty is a slur on the integrity of commerce, and a false indictment of those men, numerous enough, who are honourably engaged in trade. A man may be strong in Energy, Economy, and System, but comparatively weak in the other five. Such a man will just fail of complete success by lacking one of the four corner pillars, namely, Integrity. His Temple will give way at that weak corner, for the first four Pillars *must* be well built before the Temple of Prosperity can stand secure. They are the first qualities to be acquired in a man's moral evolution, and without them the second four cannot be possessed. Again, if a man be strong in the first three, and lack the fourth, the absence of order will invite confusion and disaster into his affairs; and so on with any partial combination of these qualities, especially of the first four; for the sec-

ond four are of so lofty a character that at present
men can but possess them, with rare exceptions,
in a more or less imperfect form. The man of the
world, then, who wishes to secure an abiding success in any branch of commerce, or in one of the
many lines of industry in which men are commonly engaged, *must* build into his character, by
practice, the first four Moral Pillars. By these fixed
principles he must regulate his thoughts, his conduct, and his affairs; consulting them in every difficulty, making every detail serve them, and above
all, *never deserting them under any circumstance to
gain some personal advantage or to save some personal trouble*; for so to desert them is to make oneself vulnerable to the disintegrating elements of
evil, and to become assailable to accusations from
others. He who so abides by these four principles
will achieve a full measure of success in his own
particular work, whatever it may be; his Temple of
Prosperity will be well built and well supported,
and it will stand secure. The perfect practice of
these four principles is within the scope of all men
who are willing to study them with that object in
view, for they are so simple and plain that a child
could grasp their meaning, and their perfection in
conduct does not call for an unusual degree of self-
sacrifice, though it demands some self-denial and
personal discipline without which there can be no

success in this world of action. The second four Pillars, however, are principles of a more profound nature, are more difficult to understand and practice, and call for the highest degree of self-sacrifice and self-effacement. Few, at present, can reach that detachment from the personal element which their perfect practice demands; but the few who accomplish this in any marked degree will vastly enlarge their powers and enrich their life, and will adorn their Temple of Prosperity with a singular and attractive beauty which will gladden and elevate all beholders long after they have passed away.

But those who are beginning to build their Temple of Prosperity in accordance with the teaching of this book, must bear in mind that a building requires time to erect, and that it must be patiently raised up, brick upon brick and stone upon stone, and the Pillars must be firmly fixed and cemented, and labour and care will be needed to make the whole complete. And the building of this inner mental Temple is none the less real and substantial because invisible and noiseless, for in the raising up of this Temple, as of Solomon's—which was "seven years in building"—it can be said, "there was neither hammer nor axe nor any tool of iron heard in the house, while it was in the building."

Even so, O reader! construct thy character, raise up the house of thy life, build up thy Temple of

Prosperity. Be not as the foolish who rise and fall upon the uncertain flux of selfish desires; but be at peace in thy labour, crown thy career with completeness, and so be numbered among the wise who, without uncertainty, build upon a fixed and secure foundation—even upon the Principles of Truth which endure forever.

James Allen: A Memoir

By Lily L. Allen

from *The Epoch* (February–March 1912)

Unto pure devotion
Devote thyself: with perfect meditation
Comes perfect act, and the right-hearted rise—
More certainly because they seek no gain—
Forth from the bands of body, step by step.
To highest seats of bliss.

J ames Allen was born in Leicester, England, on November 28th, 1864. His father, at one time a very prosperous manufacturer, was especially fond of "Jim," and before great financial failures overtook him, he would often look at the delicate, refined boy, poring over his books, and would say, "My boy, I'll make a scholar of you."

The Father was a high type of man intellectually, and a great reader, so could appreciate the evident thirst for education and knowledge which he observed in his quiet studious boy.

As a young child he was very delicate and nervous, often suffering untold agony during his school days through the misunderstanding harshness of some of his school teachers, and others with whom he was forced to associate, though he retained always the tenderest memories of others—one or two of his teachers in particular, who no doubt are still living.

He loved to get alone with his books, and many a time he has drawn a vivid picture for me, of the hours he spent with his precious books in his favourite corner by the home fire; his father, whom he dearly loved, in his arm chair opposite also deeply engrossed in his favourite authors. On such evenings he would question his father on some of the profound thoughts that surged through his soul— thoughts he could scarcely form into words—and the father, unable to answer, would gaze at him long over his spectacles, and at last say: "My boy, my boy, you have lived before"—and when the boy eagerly but reverently would suggest an answer to his own question, the father would grow silent and thoughtful, as though he *sensed* the future man and his mission, as he looked at the boy and listened to his words—and many a time he was heard to remark, "Such knowledge comes not in one short life."

There were times when the boy startled those about him into a deep concern for his health, and they would beg him not to *think so much*, and in after years he often smiled when he recalled how his father would say—"Jim, we will have you in the Churchyard soon, if you think so much."

Not that he was by any means unlike other boys where games were concerned. He could play leap-frog and marbles with the best of them, and those who knew him as a man—those who were privileged to meet him at "Bryngoleu"—will remember how he could enter into a game with all his heart. Badminton he delighted in during the summer evenings, or whenever he felt he could.

About three years after our marriage, when our little Nora was about eighteen months old, and he about thirty-three, I realized a great change coming over him, and knew that he was renouncing everything that most men hold dear that he might find Truth, and lead the weary sin-stricken world to Peace. He at that time commenced the practice of rising early in the morning, at times long before daylight, that he might go out on the hills—like One of old—to commune with God, and meditate on Divine things. I do not claim to have understood him fully in those days. The light in which he lived and moved was far too white for my earth-bound eyes to see, and a *sense of it only* was beginning to dawn upon me. But I knew I dare not stay him or hold him back, though at times my woman's heart cried out to do so, waiting him all my own, and not then understanding his divine mission.

Then came his first book, "From Poverty to Power." This book is considered by many his best book. It has passed into many editions, and tens of thousands have been sold all over the world, both authorized and pirated editions, for perhaps no author's works have been more pirated than those of James Allen.

As a private secretary he worked from 9 a.m. to 6 p.m., and used every moment out of office writing his books. Soon after the publication of "From Poverty to Power" came "All These Things Added," and then "As a Man Thinketh," a book perhaps better known and more widely read than any other from his pen.

About this time, too, the "Light of Reason" was founded and he gave up all his time to the work of editing the Magazine, at the same time carrying on a voluminous correspondence with searchers after Truth all over the world. And ever as the years went by he kept straight on, and never once looked back or swerved from the path of holiness. Oh, it was a blessed thing indeed to be the chosen one to walk by the side of his earthly body, and to watch the glory dawning upon him!

He took a keen interest in many scientific subjects, and always eagerly read the latest discovery in astronomy, and he delighted in geology and botany. Among his favourite books I find Shakespeare, Milton, Emerson, Browning, The Bhagavad-Gita, the Tao-Tea-King of Lao-Tze, the Light of Asia, the Gospel of Buddha, Walt Whitman, Dr. Bucke's Cosmic Consciousness, and the Holy Bible.

He might have written on a wide range of subjects had he chosen to do so, and was often asked for articles on many questions outside his particular work, but he refused to comply, consecrating his whole thought and effort to preach the Gospel of Peace.

When physical suffering overtook him he never once complained, but grandly and patiently bore his pain, hiding it from those around him, and only we who knew and loved him so well, and his kind, tender Doctor, knew how greatly he suffered. And yet he stayed not; still he rose before the dawn to meditate, and commune with God; still he sat at his desk and wrote those words of Light and Life which will ring down through the ages, calling men and women from their sins and sorrows to peace and rest.

Always strong in his complete manhood, though small of stature physically, and as gentle as he was strong, no one ever heard an angry word from those kind lips. Those who served him adored him; those who had business dealings with him trusted and honoured him. Ah! how much my heart prompts me to write of his self-sacrificing life, his tender words, his gentle deeds, his knowledge and his wisdom. But why? Surely there is no need, for do not his books speak in words written by his own hand, and will they not speak to generations yet to come?

About Christmas time I saw the change coming, and understood it not—blind! blind! blind! I could not think it possible that *he* should be taken and *I* left.

But we three—as if we knew—clung closer to each other, and loved one another with a greater love—if that were possible—than ever before. Look at his portrait given with the January "Epoch," and reproduced again in this, and you will see that even then our Beloved, our Teacher and Guide, was letting go his hold on the physical. He was leaving us then, and we didn't know it. Often I had urged him to stop work awhile and rest, but he always gave me the same answer, "My darling, when I stop I must go, don't try to stay my hand."

And so he worked on, until that day, Friday, January 12, 1912, when, about one o'clock he sat down in his chair, and looking at me with a great compassion and yearning in those blessed eyes, he cried out, as he stretched out his arms to me, *"Oh, I have finished, I have finished, I can go no further, I have done."*

Need I say that everything that human aid and human skill could do was done to keep him still with us. Of those last few days I dare scarcely write. How could my pen describe them? And when we knew the end was near, with his dear hands upon my head in blessing, he gave his work and his beloved people into my hands, charging me to bless and help them, until I received the call to give up my stewardship!

"I will help you," he said, "and if I can I shall come to you and be with you often."

Words, blessed words of love and comfort, *for my heart alone* often came from his lips, and a sweet smile ever came over the pale calm face when our little Nora came to kiss him and speak loving words to him, while always the gentle voice breathed the tender words to her—*"My little darling!"*

So calmly, peacefully, quietly, he passed from us at the dawn on Wednesday, January 24, 1912. "Passed from us," did I say? Nay, only the outer garment has passed from our mortal vision. He lives! and when the great grief that tears our hearts at the separation is calmed and stilled, I think that we shall know that he is still with us. We shall again rejoice in his companionship and presence.

When his voice was growing faint and low, I heard him whispering, and leaning down to catch the words I heard—"At last, at last—at home— my wanderings are over"—and then, I heard no more, for my heart was breaking within me, and I felt, for *him* indeed it was *"Home at last!"* but for me—And then, as though he knew my thoughts, he turned and again holding out his hands to me, he said: "I have only one thing more to say to you, my beloved, and that is I love you, and I will be waiting for you; good-bye."

I write this memoir for those who love him, for those who will read it with tender loving hearts, and tearful eyes; for those who will not look critically at the way in which I have tried to tell out of my lonely heart this short story of his life and passing away—for *his* pupils, and, therefore, my friends.

We clothed the mortal remains in *pure white linen*, symbol of his fair, pure life, and so, clasping the photo of the one he loved best upon his bosom—they committed all that remained to the funeral pyre.

About the Author

James Allen was one of the pioneering figures of the self-help movement and modern inspirational thought. A philosophical writer and poet, he is best known for his book *As a Man Thinketh*. Writing about complex subjects such as faith, destiny, love, patience, and religion, he had the unique ability to explain them in a way that is simple and easy to comprehend. He often wrote about cause and effect, as well as overcoming sadness, sorrow and grief.

Allen was born in 1864 in Leicester, England into a working-class family. His father travelled alone to America to find work, but was murdered within days of arriving. With the family now facing economic disaster, Allen, at age 15, was forced to leave school and find work to support them.

During stints as a private secretary and stationer, he found that he could showcase his spiritual and social interests in journalism by writing for the magazine *The Herald of the Golden Age.*

In 1901, when he was 37, Allen published his first book, *From Poverty to Power.* In 1902 he began to publish his own spiritual magazine, *The Light of Reason* (which would be retitled *The Epoch* after his death). Each issue contained announcements, an editorial written by Allen on a different subject each month, and many articles, poems, and quotes written by popular authors of the day and even local, unheard of authors.

His third and most famous book *As a Man Thinketh* was published in 1903. The book's minor popularity enabled him to quit his secretarial work and pursue his writing and editing career full time. He wrote 19 books in all, publishing at least one per year while continuing to publish his magazine, until his death. Allen wrote when he had a message—one that he had lived out in his own life and knew that it was good.

In 1905, Allen organized his magazine subscribers into groups (called "The Brotherhood") that would meet regularly and reported on their meetings each month in the magazine. Allen and his wife, Lily Louisa Oram, whom he had married in 1895, would often travel to these group meetings to give speeches and read articles. Some of Allen's favorite writings, and those he quoted often, include the works of Shakespeare, Milton, Emerson, the Bible, Buddha, Whitman, Trine, and Lao-Tze.

Allen died in 1912 at the age of 47. Following his death, Lily, with the help of their daughter, Nora took over the editing of *The Light of Reason*, now under the name *The Epoch*. Lily continued to publish the magazine until her failing eyesight prevented her from doing so. Lily's life was devoted to spreading the works of her husband until her death at age 84.